100
Text Msge
From A
President

By

PASCAL M. B. SAMA

ISBN

Hardcover: 978-1-966565-97-0
Paperback: 978-1-966565-98-7

About The Author

Pascal Bahbit Mbilain Sama is admired for his razor-sharp mind and exceptional talent. An abstract thinker with a vast knowledge spanning nursing, history, religion, politics, science, and the arts, Pascal was born in former British Southern Cameroon (Ambazonia) and raised in Nebraska. After completing high school in Omaha, he earned degrees in applied science, nursing, health management, and health law from esteemed institutions, including Bellevue University and Hofstra University.

Pascal's writing gained recognition in 2006 when his essay ranked among the top 3% in North America and was published in Authors of Tomorrow. He later served as a leading communicator in his community. Now residing in New York, Pascal is the founder of Prosperity Planet, a personal development business focusing on wealth creation through the Law of Attraction. Reluctantly, but passionately, he shares his talents and insights through his writing to inspire and uplift others.

Acknowledgment

I will not be reluctant to acknowledge GOD first for giving me the strength to write this book. Ever since I was a kid, it has been my belief there is a higher power. Like billions of people in our world today, I do believe there is a higher power. There are many names for this higher power. For example, Allah, Yahweh, Jehovah, Elohim, Hashem, The Universe, Energy, and God. Personally, I call this higher power God. If I ever achieve something great in my knowledge, I give acknowledgment to God first. This has been my promise since childhood. Therefore, I am acknowledging HIM for the knowledge, understanding, energy, and wisdom this book may offer.

I would like to acknowledge my mother, Samjeh Wilhemina Tafili Katenyin Dobgima, for excitedly encouraging me to write this book. I felt like she once gave up on my effort to write this book. She never believed I would complete the book because I was always working on too many important projects simultaneously. My mom was a teacher, and she taught English language and literature in the schools where she worked. My interest in writing speeches and using *Figures of Speech* was partly because of her being an English literature teacher. Alliteration, simile, euphemism, word repetition, irony, and exaggeration are all techniques of expression I came to understand very well due to my mom's career. I would also like to acknowledge my father, who once contributed to some minimal aspects of my life. Perhaps my uncle, Prince Patrick Sama, is the true hero I admire. He was a very generous and open-minded man. I consider him my father. He considered every child that came around him as his own. He was a father I never had. From him, I learned the art of being nice. It is a quality I enjoy a lot. He was a very nice man, and everyone I knew who lived with him loved him. He was also easy to please but very difficult to be persuaded by the things he wanted. He went for what he wanted. No one could change his mind including his two wives.

Special thanks to Ojong Asu Mirabel Oga alias Mimi Bahbit Sama. I would also like to acknowledge my friends and family around me who were positive towards my effort to write this book from day one. That is, those who always believed in me expressed it and sincerely encouraged me to write even when they did not see the future. Individuals like Tracy Michelle Haynes, Ayuk Robert Bawa, Cyprian Shila, Apelete Nomenyo, and Farruh Madrohimov are recognized in this statement. Ayuk Robert Bawa is a strong motivator from my childhood who has always motivated and encouraged me. Greetings to the women in my childhood who played motherly roles. For example, the late Mama Susan Sama and the late Julie Sama Bobyek. Special thanks to the aunty who played her role as a good aunty to me, Mrs. Winifred Timti, and her son, my cousin Glenn Timti. Consola Njang, the female cousin who has always been excited about my successes. A stretch of praise to Mrs. Bridget Ejang Fokim. I look forward to acknowledging many more of my loyal friends and family members who did not get to be mentioned here. You know yourselves. The list is endless. Thank you, *Judy Natt*, of Brooklyn, New York, for helping me re-edit this book.

My fourth paragraph of recognition goes entirely to the famous school of St Joseph's College Sasse (Sasse College), where I obtained my secondary, middle, and some high school education. Like the other thousands of ex-students from this school, my experience at Sasse College was one of the best times of my life. Thanks to all the open-minded friends and brothers from Sasse College who played their role in my life. A recognition again to my cousin Glenn Timti, who also went to Sasse College. In Sasse, the motto is *Fides Quaerens Intellectum*, which is Latin for *Faith Seeking Knowledge*.

Personally, I never wanted to be a writer. I have never seen myself writing a book but many people kept suggesting that I should write one. Every time I write an email, essay, or work report, I consistently receive suggestions from different readers that I should write a book. My classmates in college, my teachers, my professors, my work supervisors and many other personalities who read my essays have suggested that I write a book. I have so many people who have been great in my life during this process, especially in the United States. Whites, Blacks, Hispanics, Asians, Indians, and Mixed races have all been great in my experience. Special thanks to the people of Omaha, Nebraska, where I also grew up. I was raised in Ambazonia of Southern Cameroon, but I also grew up in Omaha, Nebraska, USA. My moral lessons of life came from the land of Ambazonia in Southern Cameroon but my broad understanding of the world was obtained while growing up in Omaha, Nebraska. I want to thank the people of both regions for these wonderful contributions to my life. The legal knowledge that I used to spice up this book came from my law school program at Hofstra University Maurice A. Deane School of Law. I am extending special acknowledgment to Kim M. Gill, Student Support Advisor at the Maurice A. Deane School of Law at Hofstra University, Long Island, New York. Her superior professional service had an impact on me. The nursing and medical knowledge I used to enhance this book was acquired through my nursing program at Iowa Western Community College. It also came from 10 years of working experience. Special thanks to my nurse coworkers at LifeCare of America at Elkhorn in Nebraska. More thanks again to my Omaha Community of Nebraska. With the guidance of GOD, I hope there will be more success stories to come. Again, I look forward to acknowledging many friends and family members who did not get to be mentioned here. You know yourselves. There is no room for everyone's name. Thank you all, and thank you for READING!

Contents

Introduction

This book is about a charismatic, vibrant, broken community that was falling apart in a city. A young man was called to become the president of this broken community that no one wanted to manage. The community was vibrant, influential, charismatic, and full of controversial individuals. They were desperate for leadership and unity, but there was no one strong and willing enough to put him or herself on the frontline to lead. Intelligent and competent people in the community had the ability to bring everyone together. Still, they did not dare to do it because of the nature and the complexity of the people. This young man was not afraid to take the challenge. He took the group and became the leader of the respectable men and women of the community. Against the expectations of everyone, he managed, restored, and restructured the community and the people to a path of growth and success. He was so effective, efficient and successful that the same people who had supported him to become president turned against him. Is it not ironic that the people who supported him to become president turned against him when success came? There is a moral to the story and a lesson for all of us. The author explains it to a conclusive end.

But what happened? Why did good people turn against someone who meant so much good for his people? What were the motives? Were there mistakes? Who made them? Which mistakes were made? Who did what? How did the story end? What happened?

Other questions worth asking are: what did this young man do to succeed amongst the people? What tools did he use? Would you need them? What were his tactics? Were there any? What was his message?

The anecdote of this story is not only what dominates this book. The book is loaded with *thought-stimulating opinions* designed to stimulate thinking. The book also contains broad knowledge of other topics designed to educate its readers. It contains anecdotes, opinions, history, love, proverbs, and quotes. The Author uses these things to reinforce specific points while attempting to broaden the reader's knowledge. Enjoy!

For other information related to this book, visit our website;

PascalBooksWorld.Com

Chapter 1 - Fight Broke out

I hate to jumpstart this book with a description of a fight. However, if I do not, one may not grasp the magnitude of the division that was going on. The importance of many things in life can be measured by the amount of time we put into them. The more time we put into something, the more relevant that thing becomes. I have carefully described this fight to highlight its significance in the love, conflicts, and dramas that unfolded afterward. I have taken the time to put a description into this fight that broke out in order to reveal to you its importance to the love, problems, and dramas that followed.

For a long time, the atmosphere had been tense amongst the people in the community. The tension finally exploded at their meeting on this day. Grown men and grown women talking behind each other led to a sea of misunderstanding and misinterpretation of information. The result was a fight that broke out. It is said that in life, *everybody talks about everybody*. However, it must be done constructively. That is, when we talk or speak about someone, we are expected to do it in a constructive way to build something rather than destroying something. We will find out if the talks that occurred behind the scenes in this community were really constructive. The majority of the people were hardworking, upstanding professionals. Some were nurses, nurse-aides, doctors, auto-mechanics, successful grocery businessmen, pharmacists, electricians, factory workers, and much more etc. They were working-class people contributing to society. As elite as they were, they still had one thing in common that did not help them get along. What was it? Can you guess?

The answer is MENTALITY[1] 1. Their mentality was their biggest threat. Their mentalities about one another were straining and strangling their unity. There was frustration in the community. At times, everyone appeared angry at everyone. Very few people said good things about one another. Sometimes, you could even *taste the hate* when they talked about each other behind closed doors. Again, their mentalities about one another were straining and strangling their togetherness. On this day, it erupted into a physical fight between two people.

Before I elaborate on the fight that took place at the event, I would like to take a quick moment to describe what I have described below.

As I said, those who were in this fight were educated, grown men and women with different mentality amongst themselves. Mentality is a mindset on how you perceive, understand and interpret certain things. It is a characteristic attitude of the mind or way of thinking of a person or group.

---

[1] We often confuse "**Mentality Mindset**" and "**Educational Mindset.**" It doesn't matter how educated and knowledgeable you are; your mentality can make you achieve the right or wrong solution in any situation. Mentality is a mindset on how you perceive, understand, and interpret certain things. It is a characteristic attitude of mind or way of thinking of a person or group.

Many individuals in this community did not think they should be receiving instructions from others. They felt they were equal and no one had the audacity to instruct anyone. This made instructions or communication difficult to flow among the people. Has the concept of equality become a curse to our society? How does this mentality affect us today? Does everyone really understand the concept of equality? What are the benefits and unintended consequences? What are the pros and cons? What part of the

concept of equality should we embrace? What part should be discarded? These are fundamental questions meant for you to brainstorm in your privacy. Everyone will definitely come up with a different answer.

Because of this community's mentality on equality, it made instructions difficult to flow amongst the people. The ability to receive and follow instructions is a crucial skill for anyone seeking personal growth. There is an old saying that; anyone who cannot take instructions is not fit to give instructions. It is said that while we question authorities, we should always be willing to take instructions too from authorities. It is a concept of *give and take*. We give some things to get other things in return.

More on Mentality

Assume that you are a hardworking, knowledge-able man, but you feel that women are beneath you. Assume that you cannot take instruction from a woman in the workplace. With this mentality, you will never succeed in keeping a job if your bosses are women. This mentality will hold you back despite your knowledge or educational level at your job site. Another similar example is a race-based mentality. If you are a white person who cannot take instructions from a Hispanic person, this may affect your growth in life if you have to work under the instructions of a Hispanic person. It will be very difficult for you to follow instructions and do things as a team based on your mentality. This phenomenon was what was in this community that the young president managed. This is the core phenomenon I think is responsible for the fight that broke out that day. Too many professionals in the community felt they could not receive instructions from others due to their acquired status and position. Personally, I call this Big Man Syndrome[2].

The fight took place in the basement of a house. I myself was out on the porch. Honestly, I do not

---

[2] **Big Man Syndrome: the term big man syndrome has different meanings in different contexts.** In politics, it refers to an overpowering, corrupt, autocratic, and totalitarian rule. In the context of this book, it refers to someone who feels too important to receive direction or instruction from anyone who is of the same rank as him

remember why I left that house to go outside that night during the party. All I remember was commotion as I walked back inside the house. Some teenage girls and boys at the party were sitting on the couch in the living room. They appeared quiet and frightened as I walked back into the house. I looked at them with a little surprise because they were not that way when I left one hour ago. More so, teenagers at a party scene are rarely that quiet. With my inner voice, I whispered to myself that they were acting strange. I walked through the living room door leading to the kitchen. In the kitchen space, I turned to my left and walked towards the basement. Right there, I got my answer of the quietness. As I took a few steps down the stairs, I heard a loud, aggressive, threatening, and frightening voice. "Heads will roll, heads will roll, heads will roll[3]..." the voice shouted several times. Who was shouting? Who was threatening to cut off someone's head?

---

[3] Heads will roll; Thread! Threats that people's heads would be cut off if he is pushed further.

Chapter 2 - Make the Fight Great Again

"Heads will roll, heads will roll, heads will roll…" the voice was Power Mike's voice. He was the angry one. His fists were clenched and sweat was dripping from his hairless head. His eyeglasses were hanging on the top of his nose as if they would fall off. Power Mike had been pinned against the wall by three other muscular, strong men. He was breathing fast as if he was experiencing Respiratory Acidosis[4]. While pinned against the wall, he was shouting and yelling, "Heads will roll, heads will roll, heads will roll…etc." He was in a fight, and he was ready to explode in that basement.

The fight was not between Power Mike and the three guys who were pinning him against the wall. These guys were instead preventing him from doing more harm. Power Mike had just lost his temper and punched another person. *Anger is the quickest way to make a poor decision; a wise person controls his or her temper.* No, Power Mike did not care about this proverb. He was angry, and he could not control his

---

[4]**Respiratory Acidosis** is a condition that occurs when the lungs can't remove enough of the carbon dioxide (CO_2) produced by the body. Excess carbon dioxide causes the pH of blood and other bodily fluids to decrease, making the body too acidic. The body compensates to remove excess Carbon dioxide by breathing very fast. This rapid breathing in an attempt to get rid of excess carbon dioxide from the body is called Respiratory Acidosis. *Source; Healthline*

temper anymore. He delivered an unexpected punch on the lateral side of the victim's left eye. It was a hard one, and no one saw it coming. Witnesses say it happened so fast. There were blood splashes on the wall across the room where the injured person stood. His upper left eyelid was bleeding. The area was swollen and it appeared to obstruct his vision. The sclera of his left eye was also visibly red with blood. This community in this foreign land had never experienced an event like this. It was scary! Everyone was frightened! Was this the end of the people?

There was a commotion in the basement room. Shouting, pushing, insults, crying, and yelling were the order of the moment. The crowd had dispersed into two halves. One side seemed to support Power Mike and the others were supporting the other member. As I walked closer, everyone seemed to be shouting, yelling and saying something. However, I did not understand the words which were being said, yelled or shouted. The atmosphere was full of aggression. I stood at the stairs leading down the basement, observing astonishingly. I could not believe what was happening in our usual loving community gathering. The party chairs had been pushed to the sides and on the floor. Some were turned upside down. A picture on the wall was halfway hanging. Someone had slammed into it, leaving it at the mercy of gravity. A 65-inch TV had fallen off its shelf and shattered. The owner was right there looking at the expensive Smart TV with tears of dismay in his eyes. The DJ had stopped playing music. Obviously, no one was dancing. The tune they were now dancing to was that of aggression. Everyone seemed to be at the opposite ends of the room. Some were supporting Power Mike and others were supporting his victim.

The so-called "victim" was Tricktor. That is, the guy punched by Power Mike was called Tricktor. As his name sounds, he could be tricky. He was a businessman and a well-known figure in that community. Almost everyone knew him, but not always for the right reasons. Many people liked him, but there were so many other people who hated his guts. He was indeed a very polarizing and controversial figure.

Tricktor was one of those persons you automatically know them when they are around in any gathering. We all know people like this in our personal lives. He was always trying to express some *abstract* ideas. Some of his ideas where beneficiary, others were outright *meaningless* and *provocative*. Often, his ideas were also mixed with insults towards the listeners. According to his friends, he loved attention, and he knew how to get it. Amongst his circle of friends, he was considered very smart. He dominated and outsmarted a lot of people, including Power Mike. Tricktor was always competing with someone even if no one was in competition with him. Anyone who knew Tricktor understood that he had very strong opinions on every issue. Sometimes, he uses his talents for the right reasons, and other times, for the wrong reasons. As I said, Tricktor was *thought provocative* and this was his personality in general sense. When he speaks, he creates an urge that makes others want to give him a response. During meetings and party hangouts, he had many debates and intellectual challenges from his peers. Somehow, he always got the last winning word. Tricktor understood a lot of things about life. He was also very ambitious, hardworking and financially stable. He could pay or buy a lot of things his peers around the community could not afford. Nevertheless, it was hard to praise Tricktor because he was generally a very difficult person. Sometimes, he even tell lies to pin people against each other while making himself appear to be the good person in the whole dramatic situation. Again, many people liked him and many, many people also hated his guts.

Despite the disagreements and arguments, fighting of such magnitude was not part of the culture of this new immigrant community. This new immigrant community was not Jamestown[5].

---

[5]Jamestown is a historic site in east Virginia. Historic Jamestown is home to the ruins of the first permanent English settlement in North America. It includes the remains of the 18th-century Ambler Mansion. The town is where the first immigrants settled when they arrived in USA. Disagreements, infightings, and gunshots have been linked to the early settlers' history in Jamestown.

What happened between Tricktor and Power Mike shocked everyone. The fight resulted from a long-held grudge. Tension had been building between the two for a long time but no one was aware until that day. Power Mike had punched Tricktor on this day because Tricktor had simply requested for Power Mike's email for the second attempt that night at the gathering. Tricktor had asked for Power Mike's phone number at first. He was trying to collect everyone's phone number to establish a contact communication line for the community group. He wanted to create a group texting forum. Power Mike declined to provide the number. He claimed that he did not like to be contacted by text. Tricktor had requested this contact information in good faith. He was an active organizer in the group though he had not been selected or voted by the people. He was simply trying to put his own effort into organizing the people. He was a man who had influence and he was using that to put people together. Because of his influence, it was easy for him to collect member information instead of some other persons. This migrant group had no defined leadership structure. It had no president, no vice president, no secretary, no information coordinator, and no elected leader. Like the first settlers of Jamestown, they were trying to build their new immigrant community in this foreign land. Most of their activities were controlled by

Natural Selection[6]. Those with the right talents automatically took control of the fields where their talents were needed. The migrant group was just existing in the city with no fixed elected community structure. The people met every two weeks and enjoyed themselves at gatherings and parties. As time went on, they realized the need for central communication and leadership.

Like social insects[7], humans can't function without a head or a leader. In difficult times, someone always appears to become a leader. People like this are not elected. They come to power and control through the process of Natural Selection. If you are trapped in a burning building as a group with no communication to the outside world, someone usually emerges to lead you all out of the building. In that scenario, it is up to the people to follow his or her lead or disregard it. In this migrant community, Tricktor was playing a Natural Selection leadership

---

[6]**Natural Selection**: the process whereby organisms better adapted to their environment tend to survive and produce more offspring. The theory of its action was first fully expounded by Charles Darwin in 1859. It is now believed to be the main process that brings about evolution. Natural selection is the survival of the fittest. Those who have the best skills for the situation will thrive and survive over those who do not have. *Source: Britannica Dictionary*

[7]Example of **Social Insects** are; ants, termites, bees, etc. These insects exist in communities. They have kings, queens, soldiers, and fractions that play different roles in their communities. Their manner of survival as a community is similar to that of human beings.

role. Often, his ideas were at the forefront. However, his ideas and efforts were not always met with acceptance, appreciation or kindness. Some members felt like he was bossing them around. Others felt he, Tricktor was equal to everyone and he had no authority to give instructions to anyone. There were also people who felt they could not follow his instructions since no one had voted for him. Lastly, others did not just like to see he was the one in charge. Was Power Mike angry that Tricktor was in charge? Was he being bossed around by Tricktor? Do you think he did not like to see Tricktor in charge?

Power Mike was a very private guy. He shared little of his personal information. This was for several reasons, including the behavior of some of the community members around him. Like most groups of people[8], members of this community could be sometimes nosey and backstabbing. They were generally very good people in life, but like every other community, they talked, gossiped, and backstabbed one another sometimes. Power Mike preferred to deal with them with a long-spoon[9]. He preferred to meet or hear from them once a month

---

[8] Most groups of people; in every group of people, there is a leader, there is a loving person, and there is a kind person. There is also always a nosey person in every group of people no matter the nationality or geographical location. People are just like that.

[9] Dealing with a **Long-Spoon;** is a metaphor. It's a way of dealing with people not too close to you.

when he came around the gatherings. He did not want to maintain daily contact, texting, and emailing sharing from the group. It was his community, but he did not want to mingle with them too much. He was a social person, but he interacted with others only when he needed to. When he came to the party gathering, he was always sitting at some corner in the room with a bunch of friends, drinking his beer quietly. This was his choice, but it was not healthy for the people. The people were trying to come together as one, and whatever they planned to do would benefit everyone, including Power Mike. They wanted to communicate important little information and update everyone between the week before the meetings. Others felt that everyone should equally participate to keep the community going. If a particular arrangement is to be made, it is important for everyone to be notified so he or she can prepare or contribute before gathering days. But Power Mike wanted to stay away and then come around only when there was a party and relaxation.

Tricktor was going around trying to collect contact information on this day. He went across the room, asking for everyone's phone number and then jotting them down. When he came to Power Mike, he declined to give his number. Power Mike ignored Tricktor when he asked for it. Tricktor left, but the behavior affected his pride. There was some friction between them. From what I understood, Tricktor asked for the phone number, and Power Mike said he wanted no one in the group to have his phone number. Tricktor left and came back again, asking for his email. This time, Power Mike got very irritated. He also felt that Tricktor was trying to pick[10] on him. Like I said, tension had been building between them for a long time. A simple request may be interpreted differently. Keep in mind that Tricktor came back and asked for the email in a pressurizing and sarcastic way. In his mind, Tricktor was determined to show Power Mike that he couldn't be intimidated by him. Power Mike got offended and snapped. Words were exchanged, and in a blink of an eye, punches were thrown. Pow...!!! Power Mike swung a good uppercut punch to Tricktor's left eye. Tricktor trembled, falling backward. Power Mike dived towards him again, picked him off the floor, rushed him across the room, and then slammed him against the wall by the TV stand. The 65-inch screen TV came down, crashing on the floor. Tricktor was not as tall and huge as Power Mike, and there was no way he could win a fight against him. He did the best he could do by standing up and reaching for something in his jacket. With a bloody left eye, Tricktor rolled around the floor, dodging extra kicks from Power Mike. Power Mike kept swinging his legs, trying to kick Tricktor in the ribs. Tricktor continues to roll on the floor away from him. Suddenly, Tricktor put his hand inside the left pocket of his jacket, reaching out for something that appeared like a weapon. It was a black metallic object. What was it? Was it a gun? Was

---

[10]This meant Tricktor was trying to tease him.

it a knife? Did Power Mike got shot? Did he get stabbed pride. There was some friction between them. From what I understood, Tricktor asked for the phone number, and Power Mike said he wanted no one in the group to have his phone number. Tricktor left and came back again, asking for his email. This time, Power Mike got very irritated. He also felt that Tricktor was trying to pick10 on him. Like I said, tension had been building between them for a long time. A simple request may be interpreted differently. Keep in mind that Tricktor came back and asked for the email in a pressurizing and sarcastic way. In his mind, Tricktor was determined to show Power Mike that he was not intimidated by him. Power Mike got offended and snapped. Words were exchanged, and in a blink of an eye, punches were thrown. Pow, pow, pow...!!! Power Mike swung a good uppercut punch to Tricktor's left eye. Tricktor trembled, falling backward. Power Mike dived towards him again, picked him off the floor, rushed him across the room, and then slammed him against the wall by the TV stand. The 65-inch smart screen TV came down crashing on the floor. Tricktor was not as tall and huge as Power Mike, and there was no way he could win a fight against him. He did the best he could do by standing up and reaching for something in his jacket. With a bloody left eye, Tricktor rolled around the floor, dodging extra kicks from Power Mike. Power Mike kept swinging his legs, trying to kick Tricktor in the ribs. Tricktor continues to roll on the floor away from him. Suddenly, Tricktor put his hand inside the left pocket of his jacket, reaching out for something that appeared like a weapon. It was a black metallic object. What was it? Was it a gun? Was it a knife? Did Power Mike got shot? Did he get stabbed?

Chapter 3 - Ambazonian Medical Center

Tricktor had been rushed to the nearest emergency room at the hospital called Ambazonian Medical Center. He arrived at the hospital in an Ambulette[11]. There were no Ambulance in the city to transport him. Ambulance[12] services contacted had dispatched all their vehicles that day. Only Ambulette transportation services were available. The Ambulette brought Tricktor to the emergency room in a wheelchair. He arrived with two paramedics, and there was a police officer behind him, too. The officer had been questioning Tricktor to get his own side of the story about the event. There were plenty of bloodstains on Tricktor's yellow shirt. There was also blood soaking the white T-shirt he wore underneath the yellow shirt. Both were soaked in blood around the left deltoid and left pectoris muscle areas. An ice pack had been placed and held against his upper left eyelid, which was the area of the injury. Two nurses and a nurse practitioner came out running towards the paramedics. The nurses grasped the wheelchair and wheeled Tricktor into a

---

[11] Ambulette, a specially equipped van for transporting disabled or convalescent passengers in non-emergency circumstances.

[12] Ambulance: a vehicle specially equipped for taking sick or injured people to and from the hospital, especially in emergencies.

nearby room. The Nurse Practitioner followed behind them after asking questions to the paramedics. At the door entrance, there were scattered, fresh, bright red blood splashes on the floor. They all came from different sources. One remarkable source was from the two Jewish boys stabbed by some antisemitic guys in a gathering down the street that same night. The story is too long to explain. I just know the Jewish boys were attacked because of some argument they had with these antisemitic guys. Though these two Orthodox Jewish[13] patients preferred a Kosher Oriented hospital, they were rushed to this Ambazonia Medical Center for the safety of their lives. The excessive bleeding from their wounds placed them at risk for hypovolemic shock. They had to go to the nearest hospital, which was Ambazonian Medical Center.

The blood splashes on the emergency room floor were reported to have originated from a pregnant 39-year-old woman who was 30 weeks pregnant. She was said to have experienced ectopic pregnancy and a rupture of the amniotic sac[14]. The amniotic sac is a

---

[13]**Orthodox Jewish**; is a tribe of Jewish people. They have very strict religious practices. One of their largest communities in the United States can be found in Brooklyn, NY.

[14]The **amniotic sac** is a bag of fluid inside a woman's womb where the unborn baby develops and grows. It's sometimes called the 'membranes' because the **sac** is made of two membranes called the amnion and the chorionic. The embryo is surrounded by fluid inside the **amniotic sac**.

bag of fluid inside a woman's womb where the unborn baby develops and grows.

The third case or source of blood splashes on this emergency room floor was from a 25-year-old who got shot in his left buttock. It was said that he got shot in the "ass" after he was found trying to escape through the window on the second floor of an apartment complex. He had entered the apartment to rape a 17-year-old high school student in the neighborhood. He successfully entered the complex after lying to the security guard in the lobby. He lied to the security guard that he was a relative of the family. From there, no one knows how he got into this girl's room. The TV was loud when he made it into the room. Against her parents' instructions, the 17-year-old fell asleep with the TV on that night. She had been warned several times to turn off the TV before going to bed, but she would not follow the slightest instructions from her parents. "I feel liberated doing whatever I want to do." She always told her dad. That day, she fell asleep with the volume of her TV loud. She couldn't hear this 25-year-old rapist coming into the room. She only woke up in her sleep to find a half-naked guy on her body. The guy is perspiring and riding hard between her legs. She screamed to the top of her voice as she awoke to what was happening. Fortunately, her dad was walking into the house after a long Saturday party night. He rushed into the room only to find her daughter half naked with a strange young man on her. With a loud voice, the dad shouted, "What a...?".

Bewildered and perplexed, the young man jumped to the roaring sound of the dad's voice. Confused, he dashed for the window, trying to escape from the second floor of the building. He was shot in the buttocks with a Glock 19 Gen4 pistol. The girl's father shot him as he was trying to escape via the window. The bullet sliced through the young man's right gluteus muscles without breaking his pelvic bones. This 25-year-old young man drove across the city with bleeding buttocks. He had been driving around the city aimlessly, unsure of what to do. He couldn't call the police because he was guilty of committing rape. He had left the scene, hoping his bleeding buttocks would stop. His car finally came crashing in an area around the Ambazonian emergency room hospital. He was carried by emergency personnel and brought into the ER.

The legality of the 17-year-old's father shooting this young man was in question. He was not armed and he was running away from the father. Legally, what do you think should happen to this young girl's father after shooting this rapist in this manner? On the other hand, what do you think should legally happen to the 25-year-old rapist?

It was like Lucifer flew over this entire city that night Tricktor and Power Mike fought. Across the city, the hospitals and paramedic emergency stations were reported to be short of ambulance vehicles that could transport patients in emergency. They were busy and full of different injured patients. This explains why there were shortages of ambulances in the city.

Tricktor's situation brought confusion that day. When he was punched, his entire body stumbled to the wall, colliding with the 65-inch TV. He fell down hard on the floor. From past testimonies, he saw sparks of stars. While on the floor, he put his hand inside his left pocket jacket, reaching for a cell phone. Many people thought it was a gun, but no, it was a cellphone. Power Mike's sympathizers tried to grab the cell phone from his hands so that he could not call the police, but he struggled and made that call. They were trying to solve their local community problems without involving the police and legal system. This community was one of those who believe that society is better when we self-discipline ourselves rather than relying on laws and legal systems to restrict behaviors. This concept was not working today. Tricktor called the police and the paramedics were dispatched there with an ambulette. The entire neighborhood was lit up with police lights. Police presence also made many people nervous and uncomfortable talking. Even those who supported Tricktor were not comfortable talking to the police.

Emergency Medical Treatment and Labor Act

As you can see, the emergency room was busy this Saturday night. Despite the load of patients that came without health insurance, the emergency room hospital was still required by law to treat them. Several people go to the emergency room without insurance or money to pay for their treatments. Why do hospital emergency rooms stop sending them back home even though they could not pay? In the past, hospital emergency rooms in this city would send patients back home if they were unsure of how the patient would pay for his or her emergency medical care. Why did the hospitals suddenly stop? Why do they now treat patients instead of sending them away as they used to do in the past? Doesn't the hospital lose money taking care of people who can't pay for medical care? How does the hospital make up for this loss if they treat and stabilize everyone regardless of payment?

The answer is in EMTALA. Under EMTALA, hospital emergency rooms are forced to treat everyone who comes in with an emergency. EMTALA means Emergency Medical Treatment and Labor Act. It is a federal law enacted in 1986 in response to **"patient dumping"**[15]. Patient dumping

---

[15]Patient dumping is practice which patients were moved and transferred from one emergency room of a hospital to another emergency room of another hospital because they don't have money to pay for the treatment. Patients were moved from one

is a practice in which patients are moved and transferred from one emergency room of a hospital to another emergency room of another hospital because they don't have money to pay for the treatment. Patients were moved from one hospital to another for non-therapeutic reasons. Many people lost their lives as a result of this. EMTALA forced certain hospitals that received federal government payments to stabilize patients in an emergency before they were transferred or discharged.

East view of the Ambazonia Medical Center. Image Copy Right reserved to the author. All rights reserved. By Pascal M.B. Sama

---

hospital to another for non-therapeutic reasons. A lot of people lost their lives.

Chapter 4 - Legal Reasoning

Nevertheless, Tricktor took Power Mike to court for the assault, battery, and other damages he encountered as a result of the attack. As smart and cunning as he was, he squeezed all pride out of Power Mike and his supporters. They were humbled for their own good. Legally, Power Mike was liable for the complaints and charges Tricktor was bringing against him. The legal reasoning[16] was that he, Power Mike, was the ***Proximate Cause*** of Tricktor's injury. A *proximate cause* is an event sufficiently related to an injury that the courts deem the event to be the *direct cause* of that injury. Proximate cause is the primary cause of an injury. For example, Power Mike punched Tricktor, and he fell on the 65-inch TV and injured his left eye. Now assume that while falling, Tricktor had stumbled on someone's leg before colliding with the TV. Since he stumbled on someone's leg before colliding with that TV, Power Mike may be free from being the proximate cause. If he had stumbled on someone's leg before colliding with the TV, it could have been well argued that Power Mike is not the direct cause or proximate cause of that injury. However, since he, Tricktor, stumbled on no one's leg before colliding with the TV, Power Mike's punch must have been the

---

[16] Legal Reasoning; is a method of thought and argument used by lawyers and judges when applying legal rules to specific interactions among legal persons.

proximate cause. To establish proximate cause, the plaintiff (Tricktor) must establish substantial proof that no other behavior other than Power Mike's punch led to the injury. In order to establish proximate cause, a plaintiff must establish that the defendant's conduct was a substantial cause in bringing about the harm or injury.

Power Mike's action was the source of Tricktor's harm. He was a 6 feet 5 inches muscular guy and weighed about 310 pounds. As huge, muscular, and intimidating as he was, he was also very sensitive and soft at heart. There is a theory out there that the bigger and more muscular the guy, the more sensitive he is. This was true for Power Mike. I don't know of any study that has proven this, but many huge muscular guys I have known are very sensitive. This is an opinion, and I think it is a stereotype. On the other hand, there is some truth to every stereotype. This particular stereotype was brought to my attention by a childhood friend who was slim[17]. Power Mike fits the profile of this behavior. He was muscular, huge, and sensitive. After his erratic, spontaneous, and uppercut punch, he threatened that people's heads would be cut off. But he meant none of these threats. To be fair-minded, Power Mike was not the type of person who really enjoyed fighting and hurting people. He was not really a violent

---

[17]This particular stereotype was brought to my attention by a childhood friend who was slim - Tenya Ndayong (AKA Master Planner).

person. He was just angry and very emotional that day. However, Tricktor took him to court and the law took over. It was both a criminal and a civil case. Power Mike received hospital bills, lawyer fees, and many other unexpected charges. By the time he realized, his professional work licenses were on the line of suspension and revocation by the authorities. Given his job nature, it was illegal for Power Mike to engage in any act of assault and battery. Such behavior can lead to suspension and revocation of his license in the land, which they resided. He was about to lose them due to his uncontrolled temper. The game had changed for him in the middle of the game. Just last month, he had been threatening everyone that their heads will roll - that is, their heads will be cut off. Now, he is finally realizing the impact of his statements and actions. If the case goes to court and gets trialed, he will be convicted, and his professional working licenses[18]would be taken away from him.

Power Mike was in real and nasty trouble. He never saw it coming. If he lost his working license, he would lose his home, family, business, car, status, and so many other things. Even his supporters realized that the momentum was not on his side. One by one, they went to look for Tricktor for mercy before the court date. They were begging Tricktor to negotiate with his lawyer to drop his charges against Power Mike. Legally, Tricktor had the power to drop

---

18Professional Working license could be taken away if you misbehave or have a violent criminal record.

some of the many charges against Power Mike. However, he refused to listen to the community members who came to plead for Power Mike. As manipulative as he was, he dragged the whole community and the process for months with vague responses. Tricktor always had to push the court date. The Judge also granted him and his lawyer the extension. The goal was to drag Power Mike into a lengthy emotional torment before the actual case had started. Power Mike had no choice. He would lose everything if taken to a court trial. Emotions were high and tension arose among community members. It was a psychological torture, especially for Power Mike.

One week into the court date, Tricktor made an offer. He demanded that Power Mike' friends pleading for him should tell Power Mike himself to come and apologize to him. Keep in mind that there was a Restraining Order against Power Mike towards Tricktor. He was not allowed to come anywhere near Tricktor. There was also money involved. This offer came after several months of psychological torture. Like a sad puppy, Power Mike folded his tail and went to see Tricktor as requested. He came to Tricktor's arranged location with his tail between his legs like a sad puppy. The tough guy attitude had disappeared within him. He agreed to all the conditions given to him, including the payments of hospital bills, lawyer fees, and other associated expenses Tricktor had acquired because of his violent punch. Many of his friends in the community joined to help him raise the huge sum of money Tricktor had asked for. Power Mike lost thousands and thousands of money in the entire process. Tricktor also had friends who supported his decision towards Power Mike. They welcomed his decision to squeeze every ounce of money he could get out of Power Mike for the damages he, Tricktor experienced. To some people in this community, it was a way to bring peace and order.

Mr. Tricktor had his victory, and he received all that he requested. Again, to some people, it was a way to bring peace and order to the community. Some people did not want to experience bloodier fights. If they could set an example with Power Mike, then they could assure peace for a very long time.

The incident between Power Mike and Tricktor was traumatic to the general community, but it was also very educative. No one ever attempted to punch another person again. No one punched one another in a professional, organized setting, no matter how bitter the arguments got. The entire situation was resolved, but the fight left too much tension and emotional pain in this new diaspora community. People took sides in the case, and separation kicked in. Hate, grudges, and disagreements came out of it. While some were jovial that Power Mike got what he deserved, many people became sad. Some did not like talking about it. People did not even like to recall the overall incident. The incident plunged the community into many more years of divisiveness. A community thirsty for unity was now further divided. Who was to fix this mess? Who was to bring the people together again? How could it be done? The people became more desperate for togetherness. It will take a leader to make that happen. It will take a president.

Chapter 5 - 100 Text Msges From a President

The First Text Message - Wednesday, April 17th

"Residents of the Community, last Saturday, April 13th, the members demonstrated enormous wisdom by officially reforming, redesigning, & delegating the duties and authorities of the community group. This is called CHANGE. I was chosen by the majority of the association and given the authority to be the group's president and representative and in charge of the finance handling & reform tasks. Join me in the understanding that this is a position of RESPONSIBILITY rather than a source of PRIDE & ENVY. On Saturday, prayers were said, elders gave their blessings, & champagnes were popped. While thanking u all, I consider this a "FAVOR FROM THE LORD." I did not seek it, but the burden has been placed on me. I look forward to "lead & serve you all" with WISDOM & FORTITUDE. Thanks for giving me this opportunity. Sincerely, President of the Community Association."

The president's first speech had just been cast via a text message. The newest president in town had just sent out his first text message to the community. The origins and authority of this text message came as a result of the blessings and authorities given to the young president as the leader one week earlier. A week earlier, one of the elite members of the community had called him on the phone. The young president was sitting in his room when the phone rang. The elite member said something in the nature that I need you to come to the meeting today. *"We would like to make you our president."* This was a surprise for the young man. He had just been attending the community meetings and gatherings as a regular person. He had no intention of ever leading the community or any group. He did not want to be a leader but many others thought he could make a good president. I remember when he arrived at the meetings full of life and energy. I always sat in a corner watching him. He would shake the hands of everyone in the gathering. Both men, women, and children used to be delighted by his presence. The young man had sharp brown eyes. He walked in a presidential manner, and he spoke nicely to everyone. He always had a gentle smile on his face that brought delight to everyone in the room. Sometimes, his entering to a room could be compared to President John F. Kennedy in the 1960s when entering press conferences.

John F. Kennedy was the 35th president of the United States. In his family, they called him Jack. In the media, he was called "JFK," which means John Fitzgerald Kennedy. President Kennedy's wife was "Jackie." Together, they were "Jack and Jackie Kennedy" according to the media. President Kennedy had a constant smile on his face when entering meetings or social gatherings. He was gentle and had a good sense of humor as well as temperament. He was eloquent and persuasive. However, all these qualities did not help him in his Vienna Summit on June 3rd and June 4th of 1961 when he met with Soviet Premier Nikita Khrushchev. They met in Vienna, Austria, for the 1961 Vienna Summit. Kennedy had scheduled a casual meeting with Khrushchev to discuss issues of West and East Germany during the Cold War. After the meeting, he departed the Soviet Embassy in Vienna, leaving photographers wondering why his smiles had vanished. He was crushed by Nikita Khrushchev. "He just beat the hell out of me," JFK once said. This young president of this community had the same experiences. Sometimes, he felt crushed by the strong arms in the community whom he had invited for casual, private, important discussions.

The young community president's gentle style was also compared to Thomas Sankara. Sankara was a Pan-African and President of Burkina Faso in the years of 1983 to 1987. He was viewed as charismatic, persuasive, and very ambitious. At just 33, Sankara became the president of his country and launched the most ambitious programs for ecological, social, economic, and gender change equality for his people. He was one of the first presidents of Africa who gave women full equal rights to that of men. His domestic policies were focused on fighting famine while fostering self-sufficiency amongst his people. The young president of this community had similar ambitions to Sankara. Was Sankara his icon? Did he admire Sankara? What about Kennedy? Was he an icon to this young president? Why did people compare his ways to these public figures?

What other qualities did the young president have? Why was he chosen? The answers to these questions lie deeply as you further read this book.

The Second Text Message - Thursday, April 25th

"Meeting this Saturday is at Rodriquez Wakanda. Address is below......President".

The second message that was sent to the community is here. This was the first person to host a community meeting after the young man became the president. An announcement message was sent to everyone's phone. The host, Rodriquez Wakanda lives in an apartment complex. He was very sensitive with gatherings in his apartment. He had neighbors who were very impatient with every activity on his apartment premises. They complained of noise so easily, and they were quick to call the police for any minor noise interruption. Depending on where you lived in the city, apartment complexes were rarely considered a good spot for parties, meetings, and loud gatherings. But no matter the sound level, some apartment complex buildings had sound absorbing walls. Rodriquez Wakanda's apartment building complex was not one of those. It did not have sound-absorbing walls. He was particularly concerned about the noise that would come out of his home when members came for the meeting at night. The noise would be high, especially at night. Sound travels faster and louder at night because of the Refractive Index. The refractive index will be high at night. The refractive index is also called Index Refraction. It is the measure of the way light or sounds bend through a medium like water, darkness,...etc. Sounds travel faster and louder at night because of the refractive index at nighttime.

Wakanda's concerns about noise at his apartment complex were respected by some people in the community group. Some members were determined not to be noisy while at his apartment during gatherings. Others simply did not care. They were there to attend a meeting, chat, drink some beer, get loud, get laid, and go home. Yes, *get loud* and *get laid*! There were some who believed that because Rodriquez Wakanda was hosting the meetings or parties, he should do something to keep his neighbors understanding of that particular day. They expected him to talk his neighbors into understanding that this was a once-a-year gathering he was organizing at his apartment complex. Rodriguez Wakanda was only going to host a gathering for the community once a year. They met every two weeks, but everyone hosted once a year. The people took turns every two weeks. Everyone takes a turn, and this was his turn. They expected him to collaborate with his neighbors to be able to absorb the noise that maybe experienced on that day. Not everyone had this expectation, but some people did.

The Third Text Message Monday, May 6th, 4:52 pm

"Meeting has permitted not to hold this Saturday. There will be no meeting or occasion this Saturday, the 11th. I'll be informing u all by Wednesday to inform u of the collection plan. Sincerely; President".

The meeting and party failed to take place this week. A prominent member's son in the community group was getting married. The population in town could not contain two major occasions in one day. Two prominent occasions could hardly exist on the same date in this small community. The population of the people in the community was not large enough to host two events at the same time in the city. The splitting of the crowd affected attendance a lot. On this day, the community's regular gathering meetings were canceled since no one could attend the meeting due to the wedding. But there was still a problem. Members did not accept that the meeting was being canceled. There were always complainers. It did not matter how reasonable the young president's decision was; there were always active complainers. This is part of why many people hated being this community's leader. The meeting gathering this week was canceled because of one of the member's son's wedding. Some people in the community group didn't like that. To them, the meeting would have still taken place as usual despite the wedding. The fact is that no one would have attended the meeting gatherings if it had taken place. Truly, there was nothing to be done about the cancellation of the meeting. This new community group in a foreign land did not have a written policy to address some of these situations. This community group has no written Article of Association. They have no bylaws, notes or written documents that actually describe how certain situations could be handled. The decisions the young president made were mostly out of common sense and his own personal educational experiences. There were no policies or procedures to guide him in handling specific controversial situations. Every decision that was being made was the pure judgment and reasoning of the young president and his members. It made it very difficult to manage the community group. Again, because of the nature of these uncertainties, many people were afraid to put themselves at the frontline to lead this this community. How would you like to run a community association that has no written set of rules? Every rule being followed was agreed upon orally. Member financial contributions to the group were an oral agreement, and no one ever broke the rules.

Though it was such an unstable community, they were very stable in raising money. They were expected to come up with **310 U.S** [19] dollars every

---

19 Equivalence of this money around the world can be converted as this. In Europe; 275 Euro. In Australia, 405 Australian dollars. In Africa, the currency will be 180,503 Franc CFA. In Asia, it will be 2,010 Chinese Yuan. In Central America, 5,425 Mexican Peso, South America, 1083 Brazilian

two weeks. This was a lot of money in their time, yet every single member still came up with the amount. As controversial and difficult as the people could be, they were generally hardworking people. The people worked hard in their jobs to raise money. The money was used to help fund weekly meetings and other community-related programs. Food and drinks were bought. Everyone could attend the community meetings and parties with no invitation. Strangers and friends could attend, eat, and drink as much as they could. Food and drinks were very symbolic to these people. It did not matter where somebody came from; he or she could walk into the meeting and get food to eat for free.

Reals. Middle East; 343,200 Iraqi Dinar and in North America, 400 Canadian dollars. This was a lot of money according to the standards of the day.

Chapter 6: Again, 100 Text Msges From A President

Wednesday - May 8th, 5:19pm

This is Saturday's collection address. It's the address where the heavy ongoing Graduation Ceremony will be taking place. Mr. Cho will be collecting for Lyonga. Thanks!

This message was sent out via text by the president to redirect the community on where the next meeting gathering would be. Texting the community would be the standard in directing and coordinating activities. Although this sounds simple, it was a groundbreaking thought process at the time when emails were used as a method of group communication. Emails carry huge volumes of messages and no one was preparing to read all that. Text messaging was short and easy to read. It places the message and notification in the palms of everyone. Everyone knew about text messaging but no one thought of using it to unite the people. Under the leadership of the young president, the group morphed into a mass text communication system. Again, it was a very simple solution but a groundbreaking thought at the time.

But not everyone in the community liked to be contacted by text, though it was the only practical way to communicate with every member instantaneously. Also, not everyone in this community was on the same social media platform. Everyone in the community was in the mass group text message list created by the president. It was the easiest way to communicate and connect to the masses.

There were times of backlashes of nasty responses after this young president forwarded information via text messages. A good example was from Faith[20]who rudely lashed that her name be removed from the group text list. Faith was a very spontaneous lady, according to the people who knew her. She was courageous, but sometimes, she used her courage for the wrong purpose. She had little patience and tolerance for the slightest mistakes. She was married with two kids, but one child was not fathered by her now husband. The father of the first daughter lived in the same community. No one ever talked about their personal lives, but there was something wrong with their relationship. They had a child together but never communicated as far as community gatherings were concern. I had never seen them saying anything to each other.

Faith had found a new man who came from her homeland. He was a tall, muscular, handsome guy, according to many females. He was athletic and he knew how to work together with others. There were rumors in the community that he was once arrested

---

[20]**Faith**; was girl in the community. She had a daughter with a member, but they never got married. She got married to another man and started a family life.

for DUI[21], but no one ever knew how true this was. Several individuals in the community were rumored to have been arrested for DUI too. All these were never confirmed. Back to Faith, no one ever knew when she was angry about something. It took little to strike her ego. She was one of those individuals who frightened others from taking the task of leading the community. She rudely lashed out and asked that her name be removed from the text message group. It was insulting and disrespectful. It stirred up a lot of anger, especially from the way she spoke. She always expressed herself in an oppressive manner.

Monday - June 17th, around 8:30pm

"Meeting is every 2weeks, collection amt is 310 USD, Next host collects on Meeting day…etc. We all know these things but they need to be in writing. We will call the writing "Article of Association". The president is working on it. I'm working it. Any member's input is welcome.

Thanks!"

This message was conveying that certain agreements were being put in writing. With one text message at a time, the young president was trying to make changes. He was trying to change the *Oral Agreements* of the community group to *Written Agreements*. He was creating a written *Article of*

---

[21]**DUI**; Driving Under the Influence. In this case, he was rumored to have been arrested after driving under the influence of alcohol.

Association that will govern the weekly activities of the community group. This change was not met with an applause from everyone. We know that change is usually very difficult, but for every living thing to survive, it must change. Sometimes, it has to change its policies; it has to change its relationships, habitats, friends, cities, hometowns, schools, and even husbands or wives. Sometimes, people have to change their country's nationality in other to survive. For every living thing to survive, it *must* learn to change.

There was no written agreement binding the activities of the people. The money, the meetings, and every other thing had been agreed upon orally. For some weird reason, the people liked it that way. In this text message, the inexperienced young president was trying to convince the people that the group's agreements should be put in writing.

Instead of embracing the idea, the message sparked controversy. This message was one message that caused some heated controversies. The argument was that the new young president had taken the group and immediately wanted to push his personal agendas without consulting the people. It was clear that the president wants the group to have written down information on the agreements they enjoy. This document was to their *Article of Association*. Some members did not like this. They were accustomed to doing things without official written documents and they were determined to stay that way. They did not want change though it was necessary for the group's survival.

Some people in the community refused to be part of the group because it had no official written documents validating their activities. However, many people in the group also felt that written agreements may develop a lot of legal implications and obligations for their small, insignificant community group. They liked things the way they were. They did not want to get into any bureaucracy. Do you agree with this judgment? Do you agree with this argument? Why will a community of responsible people avoid the paperwork to create an effective, solid organization? What would you do if you were the leader? How will you handle the situation? This was another challenge for the young president.

Sunday, July 8th; around 8:30pm

"I'll be calling everyone sometime in the week for opinions on ideas people have brought up to me. I'll also do a 2-month evaluation of everything about the meeting. We also need to review the common meeting greeting we first mentioned on April 27th. I'll explain this at my call. Thank u all & Goodnight!

Sincerely, PRESIDENT".

This message signifies what most people liked about this young man's leadership. He can follow up on things, especially suggestions given by other members. He makes individual phone calls and discusses with every member about certain sensitive issues. This was caring and beneficial for the people, but it was also a strategic move. It was a strategic move because it helped the young leader understand everyone at a personal level. There were many people whose opinions were not being heard. They wanted to speak, but they were never given the chance. The previous leaders did not care, nor did they have the time and energy to seek the opinions of every community member. What this young president was doing was new to many of the community members. To better understand this, read the last paragraph below keenly.

Imagine you have been in an association for 5 to 10 years, and no one in the leadership has ever spoken to you, acknowledged your presence, or acknowledged your opinion. They have never contacted you for anything about anything, they have never contacted you to issue a salute, and they have never contacted you for any of your concerns, no matter how sensitive it was. Then comes a leader willing to connect from person to person. He would hear your opinions and your concerns. He contacts you; he listens, he takes notes and then thank you for your services and inputs for the association you belong. Would that person not be a leader you will develop some trust for? Would you not feel more confident about the leader? These were some changes and phenomena this young president was injecting into this diaspora community. The person-to-person phone call also helped members brainstorm on a lot of issues before bringing them up for discussion when needed. It saved a lot of time when important issues came up for discussion. Many concerns were addressed earlier before they made their way to the general biweekly meeting gatherings. For example, I remember a crafty member who would never make enough food for everyone to eat as agreed. Everyone was expected to prepare a minimum amount of food. The community group contributed little money to aid every member in preparing food and hosting a party after the biweekly meetings. This member's party gathering was the only one that never had enough food as expected. She takes the money but never prepares enough food for everyone, as expected. Many of these issues were resolved with the person-to-person phone calls the president use to make. The president's person-to-person phone calls prevented word exchanges among members too. Once an angry member had the opportunity to express their frustration directly to the president on the phone, there was no need for them to further the frustration, problem or concern at the meeting gathering. Through the phone calls, the president made sure he addressed many problems in private before they reached the meeting gatherings. It was a successful strategy that diverted a lot of tensions on meeting days.

Chapter 7 - The Salute

The effects of the young president's leadership had grown. The population of the community group had experienced a 30% growth within 5 months of his leadership. Many people heard the good things he was doing and they came back to join the association. The young man had a real interest in the people and many could feel it at heart. He was introducing many new ideas to help restructure the community and its group. One of such ideas was *The Salute*.

Thursday, August 1st; around 8:54pm

The strength of any group or association is measured in the characters of its members. Remember to reside the "Community Salute." Our host for this Saturday is Lyonga. I will forward the address tomorrow. Sincerely, President.

A salute was a way of calling *order and silence* when someone intended to speak at a community gathering. It was also a way of unifying the people by creating a response greeting they could all relate to.

Throughout history, salutes have been used in different ways. Though usually used for communication, it has also been used to unify and create commonality among people. Countries, religions, governments, military, social groups, business associates, sports teams, and many other groups have some form of salute. The goal is to make members feel they have something in common. Even gangs have salutes and it makes individual members feel they are part of the group. Salutes are highlight commonalities among people or groups.

The proposal of a specialized salute amongst the group was the young president's idea. The people needed some new phenomenon amongst them to make them feel like one. They also needed some non-authoritative ways to call order during discussions and the exchange of ideas. This young president seemed to have come up with the solution as explained below.

When a member in the meeting gathering wanted to call for order, the word was to be yelled out, and everyone was to respond with a particular chosen word. Those words were "Compatriots and Progress" interchangeably. This is how it went; the president or some other member was to yell, "Compatriots…!" and everyone was to respond, "Progress...!". The response was expected to be strong, loud, and enthusiastic in tone. It symbolized unity. The president will yell, "Compatriots…!". The people will respond, "Progress…!".

Can you try it with someone around you now? Say; "*Compatriots…?*" Respond ...?

The word *"progress"* was chosen as a way to encourage progressive things. They say the tongue is a very powerful thing. What we speak can come to pass. This is the meaning of the word *Abracadabra*.

What we say can manifest itself in our lives. The word "progress" was chosen as a symbol of progress, which was something a lot of people expected to manifest in their lives. Even you who is reading this book now desire some progress. The word was a way to wish progress in everyone's family, progress in everyone's financial lives, progress in their love lives, progress in their jobs, progress in their children, progress in their health, and progress in their...? Add your own words.

Salutes create a sense of unity among people. It does not matter if it is a good or bad salute; salutes are generally a form of bonding. Can you think of any group you know with a salute? Complete the list below...

1. Military Salute
2. Police salute
3. A Roman Catholic Salute
4. Black Panther Salute (Wakanda Forever)
5. Japanese Salute
6. Ku Klux Klan Salute (KKK)
7. MS13 Salute
8. FBI Salute
9. Nazi Salute
10. Bamenda Chieftain Salute
11. Boys and Girls Scout salute
12. ....?
13. ....?

Chapter 8 - Salute The Controversy

Crafting a response or a salute to bring attention to a speaker was necessary. But how was the idea welcomed? As with many new ideas, the venom of criticism of this community spilled out. The idea of the salute came under attack also. It became a controversial issue. The young president's idea was embraced by many, but some met it with harsh, attacks and unthoughtful criticisms[22].

"When you are in a position of leadership, the only thing you must expect is criticism." these are the words of the great lawyer and Pan-Africanist, Professor Patrice Lumumba of Kenya. Professor Lumumba added that leadership is not a bed of roses. He said you should expect criticism and if someone praises you by chance, grab it like a platter of gold. It does not matter how bright, smart, or good your intentions are; there will always be people who will criticize and reject your ideas. This is one hash lesson the young president learned from this community in

---

[22]Unthoughtful Criticism is a common experience many of us have encountered. It is a phenomenon sometimes routed in subliminal emotions like; self-interests, prejudice, hatred, jealousy and envy. The people that usually criticize without thought to proposed ideas sometimes do so for one of these mentioned reasons. A lot of these subliminal emotions were happening in the community group. This particular chapter in this book uncovers and gives insights to the realities of the mindsets of some people in this community. The chapter also depicts and discloses the difficulties of leadership.

this foreign land. For personal reasons, some people will never accept your ideas, no matter how smart, bright, good, poignant, wise, and productive the ideas are.

Lyonga, the ex-leading coordinator of the group seemed to be the one behind the criticisms of *The Salute*. He was the one who used to coordinate the community group before it scattered and became very divided. It seemed like he was against every new idea made by the new young president. He was the previous head and lead coordinator of the group. He was not the president and he had never had the title of the president. It was very difficult for him to see another person taking control. This is a group he had failed to put together. Now, it bothered him that another person is in control and doing better where he failed. The argument is that if he, Lyonga had the interest of the community people, it should not bother him when another person is forging the community's progress. He, Lyonga should help or support the young president in building the people and the community group if he had the interest of the community.

According to feedback, Lyonga's criticism was not specific. No one could actually pinpoint what was bothering him. Mostly, he was criticizing that the young president did not know what he was doing and had no idea why the young president was introducing a group salute. He had called another member to vent his disagreements.

Lyonga; "Do you hear what this young man is saying?" he vented on the phone.

Hubert; "I heard the changes he is making."

Lyonga; "Who does he think he is? Why will he be making changes in the group without consulting the majority"?

Hubert; "Maybe it's because we have no bylaws or written agreements that say he should consult the majority. I heard that the young president said that in order to draw the people's attention while in a group meeting, it was necessary to use the salute since it might bring the crowd to order".

Lyonga; "Bold shit...! There are many ways you could capture the attention of the people without forcing

everyone to say some *salute* they don't want to say. Who does he think he is?".

Lyonga added his last phrase with a loud, angry, irritating tone on the phone. He was angry and rejected many things the president did. The frustration did not come only because he had lost power, but it also came because he was booed out of his leadership position in the community group.

I got to know Lyonga personally. He was not a bad person, but he was not sincere enough to himself. He was not sincere enough to be a leader of the people either. I think that is why he got booed out of the organization. Some said that he used his leadership position to provide special favors to his family members even when they did not deserve it. He counted votes and placed them in certain positions[23] to advance some of his family members. Lyonga worked hard for the community group in his own way. However, his alleged unjust favors to his family betrayed the trust of many people. He could no longer be trusted. Many people wanted him to leave his position as the lead coordinator. Some members of the community group were even willing to go without a leader. He was booed out. His last public speech to the group was a WARNING speech! He came and made a WARNING and a threatening speech. It was about some rumors he heard about himself. Some people were talking negatively about him. That night, he came and shouted at the meeting gathering. Everyone kept quiet as he burst out the WARNING! Some people feared for their lives.

DISCUSSION

There will always be critics but it should not discourage you. You will never realize your mistakes unless you give room for criticism. Some people will never accept your ideas, no matter how smart, bright, wise, and productive the ideas are. There will always be critics. Was Lyonga the young president's number one critic? Was Lyonga treated fairly? Was the

---

[23]Positions; he put 10th place into 1st place. He will also put 5th place into 1st place. He placed the votes of some people in the wrong place on purpose. It was said he was playing favoritism. This was what was said.

booing against him justified? Was anyone backstabbing him? Were there people in this community that orchestrated his removal from leadership? Will Lyonga come back to harm the new young president? Was he jealous of the young president? Did he plot to eliminate the young president? The drama of this story had just begun.

Chapter 9- The Ballot Box Gossip

Lyonga, the previous leader of the community group, was experiencing changes. He had lost his power and control of the group. He is not absorbing it well. There is a reason he was booed out of the leadership position he controlled. His departure excited some people, but it also made others angry. Some decided to push back.

You can always tell there is change coming when there is hard pushback on a particular idea. Often, in life, change is very difficult, but it is the only thing that is constant in our universe. As I said earlier, "for any living thing to survive, it must change." This quote was once made by Senator Harry Reid of the United States Congress. Mr. Harry Reid was a senator from the State of Nevada, home of the glamorous city of Las Vegas. For any living thing to survive, it must change. This is primarily seen in the concept of evolution, where living things morph and change their structural organs to survive. Evolution itself is another topic with a load of explanations and controversies. The change in leadership in this community brought a lot of talking, anxiety, and uncertainty, especially among Lyonga's supporters. Some people thought the president was too young for the job and or too young to handle anything that was to be handled. These were similar criticisms levied on President Thomas Sankara of Burkina Faso when he became president. His critics thought he was too young to handle the responsibilities of his presidency. This is also a direct comparison with President John F. Kennedy. Kennedy was grilled, chewed, and criticized for being too young and inexperienced to handle the presidency of the United States during his 1960 presidential election campaign. Many journalists and politicians criticized that he was too young and inexperienced to handle the responsibilities of the presidency. He proved them wrong and became one of America's most diplomatic president of all times. Like Thomas Sankara, John F. Kennedy was assassinated. Sankara was assassinated at 38 years of age. Kennedy was assassinated at 46 years of age. Was the young president of this community in this foreign land also assassinated? In comparison to Sankara and Kennedy, was the young community president also going to be assassinated?

"A society whose young men and women are in a constant state of slumber will never realize their potential," Jon F. Kennedy.

Understanding The Take-Over

This community group in this foreign land had merely existed for up to a decade. They had come from another land to start a new life in the land of *Milk and Honey*. They met every two weeks to socialize with one another. During their meeting gatherings, members brought propositions for ways they could live together as one community. They had arranged that those members of the community group would take turns welcoming everyone into their homes every two weeks. So, every two weeks, the people go to some members' house or residence to gather and socialize. In another two weeks, it will be another member, and so forth and so on...! This was a very hospitable quality that existed in this community in this foreign land. The meetings, gatherings, and parties they had were fun. There were lots of drinks, music, and dancing. After a long two weeks of continuous work, the people had a place to socialize, listen to their music, and have conversations with fellow community members from the same cultural background. Sometimes, they contributed money to fund other things, especially cooking and dining.

However, whenever any group of people come together to share their love, wisdom, and togetherness, they inevitably bring amongst them those qualities that divide and troubleshoot them. That is, when people gather for good purposes, they inevitably bring their bad habits into the gathering, which affects the process negatively. As humans, this community in a foreign land was not immune to this phenomenon. The described ongoing activities in the community needed some coordination. For example, it needed someone who could inform or direct the community where the activities would be occurring every two weeks. Someone was also needed to keep records of any activity or monetary transaction that was being contributed to fund other events. Many years earlier, Lyonga had volunteered to coordinate these activities in the community. He kept records of activities and monetary transactions that were carried out. Together with Tricktor, they made announcements about where the next meeting gatherings would be held. Lyonga was an intellectual who could handle the responsibilities of this group needed at that time. By Natural Selection, he was the head and lead coordinator. He was in his early 30s and had the energy to keep up with some responsibilities. He did a good job in taking down names and keeping records of some activities that needed to be coordinated. Overall, Lyonga did well at the beginning. Like I said earlier, he lost his popularity when the people started suspecting him of favoritism. He was not straightforward and just. This is according to the feedback of those under his coordination. Partiality and favoritism[24] was in his decision-making processes. He favored people in the group he knew and did not apply justice for all. Favoritism is in our DNA[25]and everybody is vulnerable to it. That is why human nature must be kept in check. Lyonga was kept in check. The wishes

---

[24]**Favoritism** is a form of discrimination, and it is human nature. That's why human nature must be kept in check. The word favor can carry a good connotation. In this case, the favor Lyonga was doing here was not fair for the other members.

[25]**DNA (Deoxyribonucleic Acid)** is a self-replicating material that is present in the cells of every living organism as the main component of chromosomes. It is the carrier of the genetic information of every living organism.

of the overwhelming majority of community people sacked him.

The Ballot Box Gossip

It was 12 am on a summer Saturday morning. The large part of the backyard was dark. A small sodium 60-watt bulb shone at the ceiling near the veranda. Mr. Beebong was sitting on a recliner with both legs crossed. The bulb was shining directly over his head. It is hard to miss him when coming from afar at the front yard. While the entire veranda was dark, one could see his body and his crossed leg directly under the light bulb where he was sitting. One could see his entire body, but one could not see his face. It was covered with smoke. This man liked cigarettes. He also liked to drink. He had a bottle of beer in his right hand. He was drinking Heineken, his favorite beer. On his left hand, he had a cigar he was smoking. With every draw, he puffed smoke into the air in a spiral motion. The smoke cloud goes up and surrounds his face like a huge hat. I do not know how he did it, but it was strange and cool to watch. He inhaled his cigar and then blew out a cloud of smoke that surrounded his head like a hat. Mr. Beebong was in his early 50s. He had been in so many difficult life situations and has now dedicated his life to the service of his community. He liked to be in an advisory committee but he was always afraid to take a frontline position. He was also known sometimes to take sides in problems and then switch under pressure. From experience, he does not deal well with pressure. But he was a good advisor to the president, especially in times of pressure. Besides the new young president, many other people appreciated Mr. Beebong's contribution to the community.

On this 12 am Summer Saturday, he was complaining about Lyonga's unfair handling of the community balloting. There was too much talk and gossip going on about the ballot box. Usually, the people balloted to see who will host the community meetings and gathering party every other week. When this is done, money is given to the person who comes first. Everybody takes turns in line, but some people prefer their time to come early. Lyonga's family always seemed to have the days they wanted, no matter how random the ballot was conducted. Since he, Lyonga, was the organizer of the ballots, there were suspicions of fraud, partiality, and favoritism. Mr. Beebong was discussing this with Tall Macho on his veranda while smoking and drinking his Heineken beer. The discussion went thus;

Mr. Beebong; "Tall Macho, I have seen what Lyonga has been doing. I have also heard people talking about it too."

Tall Macho also knew what was happening. He responded;

Tall Macho; "Yes, we cannot tolerate this kind of behavior. It's time for us to push this sucker out and come up with someone more faire. The community is falling apart under his leadership, anyway."

Mr. Beebong; "I would like to expose him for the fraud he is. My only concern is his respectable mother[26]. I have respect for his mother, and I don't want to bring her shame."

Tall Macho responded aggressively, "Something needed to be done. I am also tired of this family oppressing and favoring themselves in this community association."

After a heated discussion, they both agreed that the next person who should be able to lead the people was generous, non-biased, and able to unify everyone from every family. Specifically, they needed someone who could draw the younger population into the community association. Someone who could attract the teenagers, in their twenties and thirty-year-old populations of the community to come together. This was when it was decided that they should seek a young president. The idea circulated amongst many other members of the community. Support for a new president grew. He was fair, generous, non-biased, and friendly to all the families in the community. This was what people were saying. The support for the young man kept

---

[26]Lyonga's mother was highly respected in the community. She was a hardworking, productive woman who enjoyed the respect of many. Mr. Beebong and many others felt that they should not embarrass her by exposing her son's suspected corrupt behaviors.

growing. The ballot box was cast. The young president won the election and took over the leadership of his community. He was 25 years old. In my opinion, this presidential position was a lot of responsibility for a person whose **Cerebral Cortex**[27] had just finally fused.

---

[27]**Cerebral Cortex** - is a region of the brain involved in several functions; including determining intelligence, personality, motor function, planning & organization, language processing, touch sensation, and sensory information.

Chapter 10 - The Iron Will -Behind The Iron Will President

Just as how irons shape other irons into nice products, that's how other humans shape other humans into nice people. Cars, machines, airplanes, bikes, construction tools, mechanical lifts, and other iron-related machinery we use in our job sites are usually made from iron and other metals. Irons and other metals shape each other into better products. Just as irons and other metals shape each other into fine products, that is how we humans shape and influence one another into fine humans. Our personalities have a big role to play in the shaping of one another. As far as this community is concerned, it was loaded with personalities. It was loaded with men and women of unique personalities.

Starting with the young president, he had an "Iron Will Personality." Many people described him as diplomatic, charming, eloquent, and very, very persuasive. He could change almost everybody's mind. Some say that he could sell you anything. The president had a very strong WILL POWER. Though he appeared inexperienced, he had many of the natural and intangible gifts fit for ruling a people. One of those is charisma. Charisma is a trait that cannot be learned or earned. It is naturally given to those who have it. How you use it is what matters. The young president had charisma, and he understood that he had to use it to survive his people.

This is the fundamental thought process that made him distinct from the competitors in his community. The young man understood that his charisma, knowledge, and blessings were not only there for his own benefit. These qualities were naturally given to him to serve the people in his life. This was the young president's thought process. Not every leader in that community thought like that. Usually, people work and enjoy their blessings with themselves and their families. They work to enjoy the fruits of their labor rightfully. But this young president was not like that. To him, the knowledge and skills he had were to serve others. This thought process is what distinguished this young man from many of the elites who could become leaders in that community. More so, his generosity knew no limits. Financially and materially, he treated other people's problems as his own problem. There was a strong sense of empathy in this young man. Sometimes, it was mindboggling. The young man also had a sense of community and social order. These were the qualities that made him grasp the favor of the entire community. It's not that he was the most intelligent one, but that he was very caring and sensitive to everyone's problems as if it were his. Like I said, he had a strong sense of empathy. This is a quality everyone will expect from their leaders. This made him win a lot of support amongst the people in this foreign land. Giving back to your community and your people is very important, but it can be very difficult, too. However, this came naturally to this young president. He was always giving back to his community. Many people around him saw that in him. He himself did not know this but the people in his community saw it. Those who loved him shared it with him. Those who were envious kept their praises to themselves. They barely expressed their compliments or appreciation.

I must admit that the young president also had some sense of pride in him. Like many young men, he sometimes suffered the *childishness of bragging*. He was good and efficient at the things he do and everyone saw that. However, he sometimes expressed it himself. No matter how good you are, people rarely like it when you praise yourself. This was sometimes irritating to the audience. His enemies used it to create difficulties for him.

Nevertheless, the young president was still growing and maturing, especially being a 25-year-old. It is worth noting that everyone will be guilty of bragging at some point in life. Even you reading this phrase now is guilty of bragging at some point in life. We all have our moments in life when we brag or want to tell the world how good we passed that exam, how good we dumped that ex, how good we were the high school Prom Queen, how we went to the best schools, how our children are doing great and so on and so forth… etc. Sometimes, it is welcomed and other times, it comes out as arrogance.

People who heard the young president spoke judged him for what they heard, but there was a deeper story to the young man's periodic bragging behaviors. Like every adult behavior, there is a childhood story behind the president's periodic bragging. He had grown from a family where he was rarely or never praised as a child. His mother had conceived him as a teenager and could not take care of him. The young president's father was not in his life. As a teenager, his single, jobless mother and father had no means of taking care of him. The young president's uncle volunteered to raise him. His mother left to continue High School and College in another town when he was just 2-years-old. From that age, he lived with his uncle's family right up to his adolescence life. Though his uncle was loving to him, not everyone did the same. Life was comfortable but those natural affection children needed when growing up were not there. According to psychological studies, children need to be loved, comforted and made to feel secure. They also need the attention and affection of their parents. If they do not get these things, the consequences can come later on in life and they will manifest in different ways. It was reported that the young president had told some of his closest friends that he did not get the love, comfort, and attention he seemed to need when he was a kid. There was none. Often, he was insulted for little things he did wrong, especially given that his parents were not around to defend him. No one took the time to acknowledge or praise the good things he did. Therefore, according to the president, it was necessary for him to assure himself that he was strong, handsome and capable of doing great things.

He did not do this all the time but it was certainly a periodic reminder to himself. If he did not do this the negativity of those envious of him would have destroy his self-esteem as well as his mental health. Is this satisfactory reason for his periodic bragging, or was it just a young man talking?

The young president grew up as an *altar boy* in the church. Academically, he did well. He passed his school exams but no one cared. As a kid, he completed school assignments never got a praise from the adults around him. Sometimes, he was spanked and beaten for minor mistakes that did not deserve such punishments. There was always some finger-pointing for whatever he did wrong and no praise for whatever he did right. The absence of his biological parents created an atmosphere where nobody truly had his interest at heart. Certain treatments went on for many years of his childhood life but he was very afraid to express his concerns to the adults and authorities around him. Again, this went on for many years. Because no one was seeing the good things he was doing, the young man started making efforts to bring attention to the good things he was doing. For example, if he had a good score on his school assignment, he would try to bring it to the attention of everyone around him. Often, he would come home trying to share his success stories of the day. When he scored a goal in a game, he would try to bring it to the attention of his surroundings the whole day.

The young man worked even harder. With every success, he kept on trying to bring it to the attention of the adults around him for recognition. Yet, no one cared or pay attention! They were not sensitive enough to notice what was happening. Periodically, a few people will congratulate him, but for the most part, no one actually cared. Usually, only your mother or father will be interested in noticing such progress. For the most part, people really do not care if your child is doing well or making a progress. They only focus on their own. As such, this young child felt he was al one. The behavioral pattern continued for many years of his life. It became a habit that was sometimes difficult to break. Even as an adult, he caught himself praising himself and bragging sometimes. Most times, it was cute and funny, but sometimes, it came out as arrogance – which, was very hard to listen to, especially by those who envied him. It was an internal fight that many people in this diaspora community did not understand was going on with the young president. Not knowing his background, people cast their judgment for what they heard or saw at face value.

The truth is that we are all like this young president. In every adult there is a kid inside. That is, every adult has traces of his or her childhood in them. We cannot differ completely from the children we used to be. What happened to us as a child is bound to have effects on us as adults. There is enough research data to prove this. Now, I am not making excuses for the wrong behaviors that adults perpetrate. Some people know better to be better. However, I am just bringing to attention that some of your behaviors in adult life can be linked to what happened to you as a child. Everyone has some childhood experiences that affects his or her behaviors as adults. Some of these experiences are bad and some are good. It is an internal struggle we all face. The internal struggle between good and evil is what some Muslims call Jihad[28]. Again, positively or negatively, what happened to us as kids is bound to have some effects on us as adults.

---

[28]Jihad is the spiritual struggle within oneself against sin.

Chapter 11 - Kids Are Future - The Personalities

Keetoz was one of the loudest community personalities that one could not go wrong accusing him of being loud. This guy was in his fifties and was about **5 feet, 10 inches tall**[29], weighed about **160Ibs**[30] and drank a lot of beer. His stomach was somewhat round and protruding. From a nurse's assessment point of view, his bowel sounds were within normal limits. He had no pain or abdominal discomforts. He just had a protruding round stomach, perhaps from the many years of beer he drank. Keetoz had brown eyes and always kept his hairstyle short. He was an intellectual who loved to debate. He had a real love for knowledge, and he was actually knowledgeable. We do not know if he had a formal college degree but he expressed a lot of educated information. He was very educated. It is worth sharing that education[31] differs from schooling. Some people may not attend school, but they can be

---

[29]5feet and 10 inches tall; is 71 inches or 180 cm in height.

[30] 160 Ibs (160 pounds) is approximately 73kg. 2.2Ibs equals 1kg.

[31]Education; is different from schooling. In my view, education is something you learn for yourself while schooling is something they make you learn at school. For example, traveling is a form of education on its own. No matter how much schooling you get, you may never understand the experience and education traveling brings.

very educated. In my opinion, education is something you learn for yourself while schooling is learning they make you do while in school. Keetoz was very educated. He understood religion, geography, literature, history, science and politics. He always knew the names of people that average people may not know. For example, Gunther Rall[32]. Who was Gunther Rall?

Many of us use electric light bulbs today in our homes on a daily basis, but few of us remember who was behind the discoveries. Electricity is divided into two parts; *alternating current* and *direct current*. Thomas Edison is considered the founder and discoverer of *direct current*. He invented direct electric light bulbs. But who discovered alternating current? These are the questions that Keetoz could also answer. For those with a good knowledge about physics, this answer may be easy for you. However, many ordinary people may not bother with who invented what is around them.

Alternating current was discovered by Nicholas Tesla. Nikola Tesla and Thomas Edison are two giants of electrical engineering whose inventions changed history. In the late 1800s, Nikola Tesla contributed to developing the alternating current

---

[32]**Gunther Rall**, a German World War II (WW II) pilot who flew 621 combat missions. He was shot down 8 times, wounded 3 times, and achieved 275 victory combat flights, of which 241 were against Soviet fighters on the eastern front. He died Oct 4th, 2009.

electrical system widely used today and to the rotating magnetic field. A rotating magnetic field is the basis of most electrical machinery. Tesla spent many years working on a system that could wirelessly transmit voices, images, and moving pictures. Keetoz could recite inventions and stories like this.

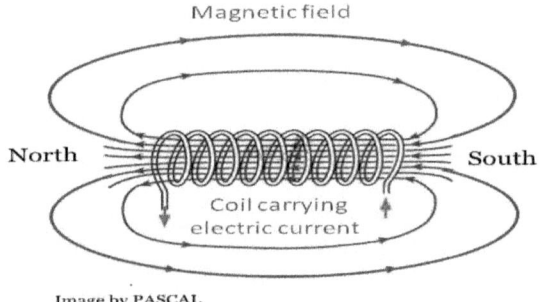

Image by PASCAL.

Rotating Magnetic Field - when electricity flows through a coil wire, it produces an electrical magnetic field, as seen in this diagram. The direction of flow of electric current in this diagram is from South to North. Nikola Tesla contributed to the development of electric current & rotating magnetic field. Image by PASCAL M

The image above is an example of topic of some complex discussions that Keetoz brought up during meetings and gatherings. The image shows electricity flowing through a wire. When this happens, a magnetic field is formed around the wire called an Electric Magnetic Field (Electromagnetic Field). The understanding of this phenomenon is used as technology in the making of many of our electronic devices today. For example, loudspeakers, headphones, generators, computer hard disks, washing machines, television, radio parts…etc. Electromagnetic field technology is usually used in scrap yards for picking up and moving heavy metals like iron and steel. As a nurse, perhaps the most significant use of electromagnetic field technology is seen in Magnetic Resonance Technology (MRI), which uses magnets to capture pictures of the inner body.

As you can see from Keetoz, this community was loaded with individuals of varying personalities and varying discussions. There is more to this;

One of the richest men who ever lived in history was Mansa Musa of Mali in Africa. According to vast historical sources, Africa has been the richest continent in the world order. Besides its vast natural and mineral resources, it also had modern-related wealth. But like other rich civilizations, its glory days came to an end. Like many other great empires and civilizations that have existed, the Kingdom of Mali in Africa was eventually put to an end by invaders. Also, *Benin Moat* or The Great Wall of Benin, Africa was destroyed by the British in 1897.

Nothing lasts forever! People always destroy the great things humanity has created. Rome in Europe is another perfect example of an empire that was once very rich in civilization. The Barbarians finally found a way to put an end to it also. These are some other topics of interest Keetoz could describe in detail. He had a very broad knowledge of science and history.

Again, as you can see, this community was loaded with individuals of varying personalities and varying topics. These individual personalities and characters also had money and influence. Many times, they compelled other community members to yield to their requests. It was very difficult to have the people adopt new ideas because of these characters and personality influences. It made the young president's job exceptionally difficult. At one time, an idea was brought to open a Children Money Savings Group for the children in the community. This idea eventually failed because some personalities did not want to support it. The others who were loyal to these individual personalities also followed them in destroying the idea.

But what was the Children's Savings Group about? Was it even a good idea? It was a very great idea introduced to the people by a man called Dr. Gangsta. Dr. Gangsta was another personality and character in the community. His idea was to be called "Kids Are Future." It was a *Children's Money Savings Plan* designed to get the children in the community to start saving money at an early age. Dr. Gangsta had approached the young president with the idea one Saturday at the gatherings. The young president highly welcomed Dr. Gangsta's idea.

Dr. Gangsta; Good evening, Mr. President. How are you?

The young President; I'm great, Dr. Gangsta. How can I help you this beautiful Saturday?

Dr. Gangsta; I have been thinking of an idea about savings for the kids.

The young president; Yes, I am listening doctor.

Dr. Gangsta; I was thinking we should come up with something for our children too. Something like a Children's Savings Group. It will be specifically for children.

The major community group was designed for anyone above 18 years of age but there was no social group for those under the age of 18. The goal of a Children's Savings Group was to teach children in this community how to save money at an early age through the creation their own community group. Many people grow up in life without having real knowledge of how to manage and save their money. We only realize this later when we are cornered with adult lifestyle and financial problems. By the time adults realize that they do not know how to manage money and finances, it is often too late. If you can teach children to get in the habit of budgeting and saving 10% of their incomes, they may have lots of money or assets saved to live comfortably during their adult lives. As a leader who wanted the best for his people, the young president had Dr. Gangsta's idea published. He introduced it to everyone and made efforts for it to be adopted.

Kids Are the Future!

As good as the idea sounds, some stubborn community personalities could not agree on anything about the project. The young president's effort to implement the program became a controversy. It was sad to see this because the majority of the kids who knew the proposed program were excited about it. To their dismay, it was never created. It was a great loss for the president and perhaps, Dr. Gangsta. This is one of those things the young president regretted never achieving. The savings group was also going to be a fun group. Gaming, play, and dance programs were to be implemented. As long as the children congregated for a group savings activity, other productive activities could always be implemented in their midst. This was the plan. Kids Are the Future! The goal was to create a program where other lessons could be fostered amongst them. However, the stubborn personalities of the community caused their disagreement to cloud the whole process. Even the young president could not get others to support it.

To be fair, several parents did not support the kids' program because they did not want to spend any additional money on their children. Some felt they were already spending too much money on their children to be creating additional savings plans for them.

Kids Are the Future; it is important to say that out loud. To understand how you may teach children about money, read Total Money Make Over by Dave

Ramsey. You can also follow Dr. Boyce Watkins Money Making and Business Investment Programs for Kids online.

Some Personalities

Benjamin Franklin[33] once stated that when a group of people meet for the shared collection of their wisdom, knowledge, and ideas; they inevitably bring with them other negative qualities bad for the group. When people gather as individuals for their good intentions, they unconsciously bring with them those bad intentions and qualities that stand to destroy the purpose of their coming together. This was happening in this community.

Again, I want to stress this: each time you gather a group of people in a particular area for a good cause, you inevitably gather their bad habits also. For example, their bias, laziness, sluggishness, disagreements, past negative experiences, envy, bigotry, ignorance, limiting belief systems, and much more...etc. I am stressing this because it is an insightful concept that prevents a lot of group associations from achieving their goals. This was what was happening in this community group the young president was managing. Strong leadership was necessary to dissolve the negative intangible

---

[33]Benjamin Franklin was one of the individuals who helped write the U.S. **Declaration of Independence** of July 4th, 1776. Though much of the writing was done by Thomas Jefferson, much of the contribution of the Declaration of Independence was from Benjamin Franklin.

qualities keeping the people apart. The young president was also very skillful in maneuvering through some of the negative qualities. He was not there to make any enemies; neither was he there to make any friends. The group was growing. Membership increased about 50% one year after he took over. That was a sign the young president must have mastered these phenomena. Some notable members have been described below;

Tall Macho was a tall, slim guy. According to the standards of the people in the community, he was a well-to-do guy. He was married and had three daughters. Those who knew him well understood that he had a soft heart. He was generous and forgiving to the people around him, especially his friends. However, he could be very arrogant. Sometimes, he put other people down for unnecessary reasons. He once drove someone out of his house at a party. It made many people sorrowful and unhappy. That day, he ruined everyone's mood at the party. Such behavior was considered a taboo in the tradition of this community in this foreign land. Because of this Tall Macho's periodic and spontaneous arrogant outbursts, many people were not so forgiving towards him. They focused on the negative part about him. This was a general error made by the entire community.

Passy: Unlike Tall Macho, he was not tall. Some say he did not drink his milk as **a kid**[34]. He was a very young man of almost the age of the young president. Passy was a very jovial and open-minded person. He could carry out very lengthy discussions with almost everyone from any cultural background. He drank beer more than everyone in the community and exercised more than everyone in the community. Though he drank a lot of beer, his abdomen was always flat, tight, and very muscular[35]. He had 6 pack! Passy was a hardworking person, but academically, he was not motivated. He was a very, very, very vigilant person. He knew everyone's personal story in the community. He knew enough to control the environment, but he liked no leadership role. Passy was sometimes very disruptive, especially when he strongly disagreed with anyone. He could be a pain in the **butt**[36] when he wants to. Overall, he was everyone's friend.

Lady Ness: You cannot talk about the people of this community without mentioning Lady Ness. She

---

[34]Milk helps kids develop strong and tall bones. Drinking milk helps the bones grow. Kids who refuse their milk usually do not attain their maximum bone height as adults.

[35]Drinking lots of beer makes the stomach (abdomen) round and protruding. "**Beer belly**" is common among many people who drink alcohol but do not exercise their abdominal muscles.

[36]Pain in the butt – is a slang phrase in American English. It is usually referred to something that is annoying.

was undoubtedly the most popular woman in the community and the friendliest, according to the president's assessments. She was a hard-working woman with an exuberant personality. Her presence intimidated many men and women. This did not happen because she was intimidating. It happened because she was equally as accomplished as most of the men in the community as well as the women. This intimidated some people. She was a smart, generous, and classy woman too. She participated and contributed to almost everyone's event. She had three daughters and a son. Men desired her more than her young daughters. She took good care of her skin and beauty. Ironically, Lady Ness's accomplishments were her greatest weakness. She was too much of a high profile and classy woman that she became intimidating to the majority of the men who desired her. She never had a steady love relationship with the men who desired her, especially in this community. She was too much to keep up with. She was also a very personal person. That is, she kept her relationships and private life to herself. It was not in her personality to disclose the things that bothered her, especially at a very personal level. Due to her profile and attitude, it was necessary for her to travel out of that community or city to find the man of her love.

Kambas was an extremely boisterous guy. He liked exercise and weightlifting. He was very strong and muscular. He liked taking off his shirt to show off his muscles. The girls liked it, but the guys despised it. To many guys, his behaviors were comical and laughable! Kambas was too boisterous, and sometimes, it could be irritating. He was the guy who went to an official party and then took off his shirt after being too excited. Like most people, he liked attention. It could also be argued that he liked attention more than the average person. Nevertheless, his presence made many people laughed.

Mr. J; he was as tall as Tall Macho but he was more muscular. He was also married with three kids. Mr. J was an intelligent man and a very collaborative guy in the community. He did not look down on some people as some elites did. He and his family attended and supported all major events that needed his support. He liked sarcastic jokes and he was indeed funny! From every assessment, Mr. J could be a good leader but he was not a very courageous person. That is, he did not like to expose himself to a certain level of criticism. He was very sensitive and disliked public confrontations. He did not have the thick skin to absorb unconstructive insults that came from the community. He worked as an adviser. In all analysis, he was good in his role as advisor. Life circumstances came; he took his entire family out of the community and moved away to another land.

Chapter 12 – The Sexual Energy in the City

There is no group of people in a land, village, city, state, country, or continent that can exist without sexual activities. Sex is life by itself. It is the instrument of creation, which our Creator created. The forces of sexual desires are so strong that we, as humans, cannot suppress them. Sexual desires can only be controlled; they cannot be completely suppressed or eliminated. It is part of the reason why sex is one of humanity's oldest betrayals. This is because of the strong natural desires that surrounds sex. It is often said that all problems in the world revolve around three things: Money, Power, and *Sex*.

If you don't talk to your children about sex, they will eventually grow up to learn it from someone else. If they learn it from someone else, they may not learn it the way you wish them to learn. They may learn about sex in ways that will make your brains and hearts ache. Many of us fail to teach or talk to our children about sex. Communities and societies that preach extreme suppression of sex only end up in scandals and rumors of unbearable sexual accusations. Catholic churches have suffered scandals of priests and sexual abuses. To some people, this is partly because of their rejection of priests from getting married and having sex. There is a lot to discuss about this topic, but I am not an expert on it. There are many reasons for the sexual scandals in churches, but I am not an expert on this topic.

Muslims Imams and Buddhist Monks have also suffered scandals of sexual abuses too. To some people, this is also partly because of their suppression of sexual expressions. This phenomenon has also been reported in some mosques though it is generally kept quiet for fear of repercussions. I met a woman in Long Island, New York from the Middle East who expressed the staggering rape incidents in the region. Due to very strict Islamic laws, sex is highly suppressed in the Middle East and other Muslim dominated regions of the world. Dress codes are designed to discouraged expression of beauty. Sexual expression is extremely frowned upon and forbidden. Since sexual attraction and expression can only be expressed and cannot be completely suppressed, a lot of people in these regions look for other ways to release that energy (sexual energy).

In this community in this foreign land, sexual activities existed among members, though it was hidden. Everyone was sleeping with someone. Oh yes, I said it; everyone was having sex with someone! However, it was usually respectful and consensual. Biweekly parties gave room for people to meet new lovers and have sex. Some even found their wives and husbands in these party gatherings. Others found their partners. Sex and sexual language were not expressed more often in the open, but it was happening behind the scenes. It was encouraged to be discussed only amongst the adults. Even the school districts in the land were having a heated debate on when schools should teach children about sex. Religious affiliates clamped on the notion that sex before marriage was a sin. Science-oriented individuals clamped on the notion that sex is a natural phenomenon of the creator designed to procreate. The outcome of this argument was a mess. Sometimes, the young president, who hardly kept his opinion to himself, was forced to be quiet when the debates started in the local community gatherings.

Married or non-married, sex can be seen as a means of life's way of hanging onto life from one generation to another. Sex creates offspring, which is nature's way of hanging on to life. It can be argued that your children are not really your children. *They are nature's way to hang onto life*[37]. The death rate around the world is so alarming that there is a need for rapid reproduction and replacement of life. If not for sex, especially before marriage, the earth's population would have been wiped out. Think about

---

[37]Your children are nature's way of hanging onto life from one generation to another. This phrase came from the great Lebanese poet and artist Khalil Gibran. He is best known for his classic 1923 book The Prophet. Gibran wrote great insights about loss. According to him, the possibility of sorrow or disappointment is what can uplift the human spirit to heights of happiness. According to Gibran, your children are not your children. They are the sons and daughters of life's longing for itself. You are the bows from which your children, as living arrows, are sent forth into life

it! If not for sex before marriage, it is believed that the earth's human population would have been extinct. In 1999, the United States Institute of Medicine published that 98,000 people die in hospitals each year because of medical errors that could have been prevented. Their estimated conclusion came from two major studies. With the increase in technology, it was later found that the 98,000 number of people who died per year was an underestimation. Today, the *estimated number* [38] is around 440,000 per year. These numbers disclose the rate at which people die per year. There is a rapid need for population to be replaced. The argument is that if humans have to wait until marriage before having sex to produce offsprings, the population on earth may be extinct. Keep in mind that the 440,000 deaths per year are only in the United States and does not constitute other nations. More so, the mentioned 440,000 deaths in the United States do not include deaths caused by cancer, heart disease, motor vehicles, gunshots, and more...etc. These entities have their own number of people per year they kill in the United States. This makes the number of death higher than 440,000.

Furthermore, we have not included the number of people who die per year from diabetes. Diabetes mellitus is a major cause of blindness, according to

---

[38]This estimated number is published by the Leapfrog Safety Group Grade, which is a not-for-profit organization dedicated to the research of hospital safety.

the World **Health Organization**[39]. It also causes kidney failures, heart attacks, strokes, and lower limb amputations. In 2016, an estimated 1.6 million deaths were directly linked to have been caused by diabetes. 2.2 million deaths were attributed to high blood sugar. If we have to wait until marriage before having sex, the earth's population will be extinct. This brings awareness to the variations of our sexual customs. It is based on our thought processes. It is now understandable why different cultures have different sexual customs.

Sexual Energy is the most persuasive energy humans can have and it is to be used responsibly. The more sexually appealing you are, the more likely you can persuade or win favor from the opposite sex. This is the science that millions of companies around the world explore today. Airline flight attendants are usually viewed as sexually appealing. The most successful salespersons in the world are usually physically and sexually appealing. According to Dr. Boyce Watkins, an PHD finance professor and founder of the online Black Business School, studies have shown that women are very attracted to rich and powerful men. Women find these men sexually attractive. Likewise, most men are very attracted to good looking attractive women. It does not matter to

---

[39]**Diabetes**– World Health Organization (WHO); https://www.who.int/news-room/fact-sheets/detai/diabetes.

the men if the woman is rich, poor or average – what matters is if she is beautiful.

Sexual energy is entirely another topic on its own. It might benefit you if you understand it. Some cultures discourage sexual discussions, especially at an early age. Though this is reasonable, many of their adults grow up without understanding the enormous influence sex and sexuality have in our lives and minds. As adults, sexual energy or sexual attraction is a topic that must be understood. This is because of the effects sex and sexuality have on the lives and minds of young adults. Understanding sexual energy or sexual attraction can not only improve your relationships, but it can also effectively help you manage your family, businesses, schools, work environments, churches, sports teams, and many other environments.

The saying is that; "learning, learning without playing, makes Jack a dull boy" is very true. We have to have some fun in our lives to effectively function in the more important things we need to do. This community in this foreign land had its fun times. Everyone was having sex with their partners, wives, husbands and there were little or no sexual scandals. The energy was properly released!

The Sexual Scandal Suspicion

I do recall that a sex scandal was to erupt. It was about Dr. Gangsta's wife. There was a fight that night at home between Dr. Gangsta and his wife. The police were called. Fearing complications, the couple hid the problem from the entire community. According to sources, Dr. Gangsta was suspecting his young gorgeous wife was having an affair with the young president. That night at the party, his attractive young wife was conversing with the president as many others did. At some point, she drank from the glass the president was drinking from. Dr. Gangsta had been watching the two of them across the room. He saw what had happened. His suspicions and jealousy grew when he saw his wife sipping from the young president's non-transparent glass. I would be angry, too. Would you? It was not clear what the conversation was about, but his gorgeous young wife stretched her hands, grabbed the president's glass and then drank from it. The young president had offered it to her. According to feedback, there was a bitter quarrel at home that night. The incident eventually turned into a fistfight. A neighbor was concerned and the police were called.

The couple already had their problems way before his wife drank from the president's glass. Whatever happened later was just a catalyst of release of anger. It was a mistake for Dr. Gangsta's wife to sip from the president's glass, especially to the viewing of her jealous husband. Every suspicion that had been going on seemed to explode that night. The irony is that a man who has an affair with another woman is less likely to have a drinking conversation with the woman at the viewing or sight of her husband. A person who has an affair with another man's wife rarely has a conversation with that wife in the open at a party around the man. Usually, people with such sexual affairs avoid discussing where one of the other partners could be watching. A reasonable and abstract thinker understands this. The whole suspicion did not make sense to many people. Did Dr. Gangsta have another motive for quarreling with his wife? Did the wife actually have an affair with the young president? Was she attracted to the young president? Did the young president seduce the wife? Did they like each other? Was the wife a cheat? Was the young president a womanizer? There are many opinions on this but the answers to these questions are along the lines of the reading.

Sexual Preferences – Homosexuality or Polygamy

This community in this foreign land was not ready for some sexual preferences that developed amongst them. Like many communities at the time, this community struggled with the acceptance of homosexual and polygamous relationship preferences. Which of these non-traditional marriages would you prefer, **homosexuality or polygamy**?

Two girls in the community started liking each other. They liked each other and started dating. They started dating, kissing, and having sex. No one saw it coming, includeing their beloved father. Homosexuality was like a taboo amongst the people, but it was also a human behavior they recognized existed.

Though it was a known, recognized sexual orientation, it was not fully embraced in this community. Out of 100%, the acceptance level was about 50%. The lesbian girls were identical twins. They were nice, cooperative, open-minded, and well-liked. Their sexual preferences were what set them apart from other young girls in the community. They were not treated any differently because of their sexual preferences. They walked around freely and did what they wanted to do in private. These girls did not want to be females. Mentally, they acknowledged to the president that they did not feel like females. They felt they were trapped in the wrong body type. It was who they were. This raised a big question, which is *Nature vs. Nurture*. Are people the way they are because of the influence of their environment, or they are who they are because of their genes? Are people born gay, or do they learn the behavior from the environment in which they grew up?

The two girls wanted to be males and it was evident in their lifestyles. They received **testosterone**[40] hormonal injections, which helped enhance their masculine characteristics. They lived their lives ignoring any judgmental attitudes from anyone. As far as I know, they were accepted for who

---

[40]Testosterone is the hormone responsible for male sexual character traits such as; deep voice, Adam's apple, increase muscle mass... etc. The opposite of testosterone is estrogen. Men have more testosterone while females have more estrogen; hence, the reason for male and female sexual characteristics.

they were. Though there were people who did not accept these girls' sexual orientation, few people in the community talked about them. It was a subject that everyone had an opinion about, but no one took the time to make it a subject to discuss. The lesbian twins were just living their lives like every other human. They were happy, and life went on.

Sexual Preferences – Homosexuality

Homosexuality was once seen as a medical diagnosis. According to the fourth edition of the **Diagnostics of Statistical Manual of Mental Disorders**, it was a medical condition diagnosed and treated. That is, it was taught in medical schools as a disease, and it was treated in hospitals as a medical problem. **Conversion therapy** was prescribed as treatment. Today, this "dogma" has changed. Even the statutes and laws that made homosexuality a crime have all been strapped off the book. It is usually said that a society's laws reflect its values. As the values of a society change, that is how its laws change too. Look back at the change of our laws in the United States for the past 50 years. Gay Rights, Civil Rights, Women's Rights, Disability Rights, and more...etc. These classes of people did not have certain rights some 50 to 100 years ago. The society did not think they had certain rights. The laws of that time reflected this opinion. Our laws today highly protect these categories. Gay Rights, Civil Rights, Women's Rights, Gender, National Origin and Disability Rights are now protected. This is a clear change in our value system as a nation and it is reflected in our laws today in the United States. Again, as the values of a society changes, the laws of that society change too. What is viewed today as wrong may be acceptable tomorrow as correct and what may be acceptable today as correct may be viewed as wrong tomorrow.

Cultural Dilemma – Homosexuality vs. Polygamy

Some people really think there is no such thing as homosexuality in their culture, land, community, city, or country of birth. One guy once argued that there are absolutely no homosexuals in his country of Saudi Arabia, given the strict religious laws. The truth is that there is every personality in every group of people in every part of the world. For example, there is always a leader in every group of people, there is always a jokester in every group of people, and there is always a thief in every group of people. These character personality traits will always be found in every society or group of people. Just as how this character personality phenomenon exists in every group of people, that is how homosexuality exists in every group of people.

Polygamy[41] is the practice of marrying multiple spouses. It is the practice or custom of having more

---

[41]Polygamy – The practice of marrying multiple spouses. It is legal in some countries that homosexuality is illegal. *Source Wikipedia.*

than one wife or more than one husband at the same time. Which of these non-traditional marriages would you prefer to be legal? Homosexuality or Polygamy? Which will you prefer? Can you change people from practicing these sexual orientations? Can you change a person's sexual orientation? These were some questions in the debates that took place in this community. It is also a question that is being asked today in many countries around the world.

Unlike homosexuality, polygamy is illegal in many Western countries. But it is legal in some non-western countries. There is an underground debate between polygamy versus homosexuality. It is a debate in which many people from both countries that legalize these forms of marriage have not made the connection. At least, the debate has not reached the national level. There is a similarity between homosexuality and polygamy. This statement may bamboozle you, but there is truth to it. I am comfortable to say that the *average American Mind* is extremely disgusted by the thought of polygamy. From experience, our American women are particularly disgusted by the thought of it. In fact, it is illegal, and you can get thrown in jail for it. This is where the correlation comes with homosexuality. Just as how irritated and disgusted we are about polygamy, that is how other people in other countries are irritated and disgusted by homosexuality. In fact, homosexuality is illegal in many countries, and you can get thrown in jail for it too. Just as how you can get rejected and locked up in America for practicing polygamy, that is how you can get rejected and locked up in other countries for practicing homosexuality.

The million-dollar question is: *can we change a person's sexual orientation*? Who is correct? Who is wrong? Should governments be making laws determining our sexual and marital preferences? Why should women be allowed to marry other women, and then two other women are denied from marrying one man? Why should a man be allowed to marry another man, and then two other men are denied from marrying one woman? Assume that they all consent to it. Should it still be illegal? These are some of the questions and debates that took place in the community meetings and gatherings. Again, Keetoz was always at the center of such intellectually controversial topics. As we can see, sexuality is a very complex topic. It has so many components to it. Personally, I am not an expert. There are resources out there to help you dig deeper into this topic.

It would be unfair to close this chapter without talking about the most sexually desired person in this community in a foreign land. From the president's assessment, Kambas was physically the most sexually desired male, while Lady Ness was physically the most sexually desired woman. Many women desired Kambas, though they never made it public. Lady Ness was an eye *candy*. She had a curvy shape, smooth long legs, a round butt, and a huge significant breast. This woman understood how to use her sexual energy. Perhaps that is because she was very appealing to many men around her. She was very intimidating to women because the husbands of these women openly flirt and desired her. They could not help themselves!

Chapter 13 - The Peak

The community had grown under the leadership of the young president with the efforts of other members. Success was recorded at an all-time high. People who had left the land came back to attend the biweekly meetings and gatherings. Morale was high, and everyone was excited. In fact, the people were happy. There were parties, music, and a sense of togetherness. This was the peak of the young man's accomplishment as president. He had articulated many sincere text messages that finally sipped into the consciences of the people. He urged them to ignore their differences and focus on what they have in common. His words were charismatic and easy to read. Everyone was reading and understanding his good intentions. Good people joined him in support of his efforts. The machine of progress just kept rolling and rolling. The people were coming together, and they were experiencing **Good Times**[42] in their lives.

---

[42] Good Times; the people were enjoying their time together.

Chapter 14 - The Community Cheated Death

How did the community cheat death? What happened? Was there another fight? Did Power Mike lose his temper again and break someone's mandible bone? Did someone cheat and then run with the entire community's life savings? How was the problem handled? Did someone die?

How the community cheated death came while the group was having a party dinner one Saturday night at the home of Tall Macho. After all the fun, parties and laughter we experience in life, the grim realities of life always occur. On this Saturday night, there were food and drinks, and everyone was dishing and eating at Tall Macho's house. As usual, no one was to pay to eat. That was the verbal agreement in the community group parties of the land. Everyone had their turn in cooking meals and buying drinks for the people. That day, the party was in the home of Tall Macho. The music was booming; the house was full of people, energy, and excitement. The kids were running around, playing and having fun. Boys and girls cornered themselves in corners with the latest news of the week. Debates and controversial issues of the day were usually common during certain community party gatherings. It was fun to listen to the different news items and different opinions. Donald Trump's presidential campaigns were notably a boiling debate. His name brought happiness, disappointments and bitter arguments. Vladimir Putin of Russia, Europe, China's world dominance, Israel and the Middle East, Africa Sahel States, Artificial Intelligence, Hip Hop sex scandals and more topics... etc.

President Paul Biya of Cameroon, Africa was a dictator people talked about too. He had been in power for 41years. How did he manage to stay that long in power without an uprising from his people? The answer to this was deeper than many could answer. To me, whenever one person in a country grows too powerful that he or she starts oppressing the rights of every citizen, the people in that country have *only themselves to blame*. That is, if a president in a country ever becomes too powerful that he or she starts controlling the courts, the legislators, the military, the police, and the rights of every citizen, the people of that country have *only themselves* to be blamed. No one should be allowed to have any such absolute power. Even the nicest and kindest person in the world becomes corrupt when given such an absolute power. For power corrupts and absolute power corrupts absolutely.

Again, how did the community cheat death? What were the hard, grim realities of life that occurred?

Please continue to read below . . .

On this day at the party, the young president had walked up to the food area around 6 pm. He grabbed a plate and glanced at which of the finest foods he had an appetite for. There was a lot to eat at the party events. I mean a lot. The president went around the first table and did not find anything interesting to eat. He went to the second table and saw what he was looking for. He filled his plate with some healthy combination of food he liked. This guy eats a lot, and his appetite is ready for the load of food on his plate. He had a drinking glass in his right hand. The glasses or containers the young president drank from were never transparent. He drank from a nontransparent cup or glass so that no one recognized what choice of drink he was drinking. You never know if he was drinking water, juice, wine, beer, or hard liquor. The question is, what would you want your president to drink at a dinner party? This is the mindset the president created amongst the people. No one knew what he drank because you could not see through his drinking cup. Leader affects the behaviors of a society and it trickles down to the average individual. Good or bad, people mimic the behaviors of many of their leaders. A president who drinks a lot of beer will likely get a lot of his people drinking lots of beer. An example of this phenomenon was seen in Tupac. **Tupac Shakur**[43] was a talented, proud thug. Most

---

[43]Tupac Amaru Shakur; is a famous American rapper, artist, and movie actor in the 1990s Tupac was also known by his stage names 2Pac or Makaveli. He is considered by many to be one of the most influential and greatest rappers of all time in the hip-hop industry. He promoted a thug lifestyle as a

young men who followed him in the 1990s liked the thug lifestyle he projected. This affected their way of life. Some of the young men became rappers, too, in their private lives. The behaviors of the leaders or icons around us do have an effect that trickles down to the common individuals. The young president understood this. He prevented other young men from knowing what he was drinking to prevent them from drinking a lot of alcohol, which can be bad for them. Alcohol is good in moderation, but it has a load of problems that come when consumed excessively or regularly. Alcohol does mimic the effects of diabetes insipidus[44].

Again, what happened? What were the hard, grim realities of life that occurred to wake up everyone in that community? How did the community cheat death? Please continue to read below . . .

As the young president walked two steps away from the table with his loaded food plate, Tall Macho's wife stepped to his side suddenly. She was

---

symbol of the ghettos he grew up in. Tupac was shot and killed in Las Vegas in 1996. His killer is still unknown.

[44]Diabetes Insipidus is a endocrine hormonal problem where the brain stops producing hormones that help a person reabsorb water. This hormone is called antidiuretic hormone and it is the hormone responsible for helping your body reabsorb or retain the water you put in your body. When the brain stops producing this hormone, individuals urinate constantly and become dehydrated. Treatment is done with lifetime of hormone replacement and rehydration.

about 6 feet, 2 inches tall. There is a lot to say about her, but we cannot too detail about her. However, she was one of the pioneers of the community. She was one of the first immigrant persons that belonged to the community group. She was an active community member with a long history of support for the community, but she had a bad reputation amongst her friends because she did not treat them nicely. According to many, she was not fair to them. Personally, I do believe this! This is because her loyalty was with her family. She was so obsessed with supporting her family that she often failed to give *justice* to others in the community who deserved it. That is, she will support her family at all times even if they are wrong. She also had a weak temperament and was quick to anger. For example, she will call and harass other women on issues she felt she was correct. She was also a well-accomplished woman, but she could be too stubborn. Some people ignored her bad behaviors, but others were not so forgiven. The young president was there to serve everyone, so he did not care or fed into these sayings. As long as her behavior did not interrupt the community's agendas, the young president stayed away from their female matters.

Tall Macho's wife had a meal plate and a fork in her hands. As she approached the president from the left side, the president looked at her and smiled. The president greeted her and walked another two steps away from her. She called out three times;

Tall Macho's Wife; "Mr. President, Mr. President, Mr. President…I just want to tell you what I told another member just now."

The President; "life is full of surprises, but please, go ahead."

Tall Macho's Wife; "it's my place to inform you that someone has been diagnosed with leukemia in this community."

She told the president that one of the community members was diagnosed with leukemia. His name was Zayston. He was one of the nicest and calmest individuals you could have for a friend. He was tall, muscular and did not like confrontations. Unlike many others, Zayston never talked about people. If he did, it was something neutral. Zayston was a soft speaker though he could be loud in exciting discussions. Like any human, he got angry but it was difficult to see him angered. He had a good sense of humor, and he knew how to make people laugh. He was married, but the girls still loved him a lot. Zayston had a good wife. She spoke English but she also spoke her native language, which was French. Together, they had two kids under the age of five. They had a small new nuclear family they were trying to grow. Everything came to a halt with Zayston's diagnosis.

According to the American Cancer Society, Leukemia is a cancer of the early blood-forming cells. It is cancer of the body's blood-forming tissues, including the bone marrow and the lymphatic system of the body. Most often, leukemia is a cancer of the white blood cells, but some leukemia starts in other blood cell types. Leukemia can be fast-growing or slow growing. It is the most common cancer in children and teens, accounting for almost 1 out of 3 cancers. Zayston was not a child or a teenager. He was in his early forties and here he was diagnosed with the disease. This was rare. Very rare!

Chapter 15 - The Community Cheated Death Again

Zayston's cancer diagnosis was like a death sentence. His wife was to be left with his two kids, home mortgage, car payments, light bills, electric bills, medical costs and many other responsibilities that comes as a widow. Based on the living standard of the land, she would not survive on her own without help. She would not survive without outside community help. She needed extra hands so she could stand on her feet when he was to be gone.

The decision to raise money to support Zayston and his family was to be made by the young president to whom the community group had given the authority. After consulting the ideas of some other members, he was to decide for a fund-raising support for Zayston. The people have always lived with each other in this foreign land but have never experienced such a serious medical diagnosis amongst any of them. The new immigrant group had no protocol for handling such matters. Everyone was struggling. The announcement was made at the party that night, and the atmosphere turned into a very sad one. There were no shortcuts. The announcement was publicized that Zayston was diagnosed with a rare form of cancer for his age, Leukemia. In the minds of many, it was clear someone was dying. Many people cried that night after hearing the news. One member slammed his head on the wall in sorrow and pain. It was his own way of expressing his grievances. Another member was leaning against the wall with his back in an upright position. After hearing the news, his wine glass dropped out of his hand. His knees bent forward, and he slid to the floor in a sitting position. He then bent his forehead over his knees and cried. Several individuals were rolling on the floor with loud cries. The young president himself lost his appetite to eat the food he had loaded on his plate. He was a young man who ate a lot. He could eat very large portion of food. This day, his appetite had disappeared. He had no sense of smell or taste after hearing the news of Zayston's diagnosis.

Zayston's cancerous diagnosis was a tragedy for the community but it was even worse for the young president. Why was this?

As an ordinary person, some decisions seem simple, but when you are in a leadership position, simple decisions become more complex. The young president was caught in a tragic situation and also a complex, controversial situation. As good and nice as Zayston was, he never participated in supporting this community. Before he got sick, he was not an active member in the community affairs. Him and his wife did not attend or participate in many community members' events as expected for support.

Zayston and his wife used to attend community gatherings in support of the community but for several years, they had stopped coming. They lived a secluded lifestyle, especially right after their marriage. For many years, they did not interact with other people. They did not dispense reasonable amount of energy towards improving the community's needs, especially when others needed them. Though not as severe, other people had fallen sick before Zayston. Many people had organized ceremonies, and some others had experienced situations that needed community support but Zayston and his family were never really around to support. For some personal reasons, they did not mingle a lot with the general community for a long, long time. For all these reasons, some people did not feel Zayston and his family had done enough for the people to support him, especially in this difficult time. These were reasonable complaints, given the circumstances. Some people felt the community group should use this situation as an example against individuals who do not patriciate but need help in times of tragedies.

Despite the different positions of many people, no one attempted to raise the complaint verbally. There was a time for everything and this was not the time to raise such complaints according to many. People questioned what was happening but the discussion and dilemma went on behind the scenes. For individuals to survive, it is essential they live in a community. If the community dies, individuals lose and eventually die. If the community survives, individuals survive and everyone wins. Every individual lives in a community and every individual has some responsibility in taking care of that community. When individuals support and take care of their community, the community in return supports and take care of the individual. It is a symbiotic relationship, but this was not the case was Zayston. He was never there to support his community, but now he may need the community to support him and his family. If you want to live in a clean house, you must take care of that house. This is true for your community. If you want to live in a nice, organized community, you must take care of that community. This community in this foreign land relied on each individual to grow themselves.

Tension was building up. Given his leukemia diagnosis and out of work, Zayston really needed help. This was no joke; it was reality. What will the people do? What will they decide? Did they abandon Zayston? What will your own people do? If you were the young president, what would be your decision?

Chapter 16 - Absolutism vs. Relativism

The community people's decision to support Zayston under the young president was made on moral grounds. Every group of people will handle this same situation differently. The decision to assist a person who is dying is sometimes influenced by the level of support that person has provided in your life. The decision to be made by individuals in this situation may also be based on their cultural, religious, or ethnic backgrounds. This can fall under the moral concept of Absolutism vs. Relativism. Ethical absolutism versus ethical relativism. Which one of these moral guides should society use for making moral decisions? Should we use Moral Absolutism, Moral Relativism, or something in between?

Ethical Absolutism means that some actions are wrong or right no matter where in the world the action takes place. It is the presence of universally applicable moral questions, valid for all people and all times. The whole concept of ethical absolutism is that some decisions or behaviors are wrong no matter which community or country the behavior took place. But **Ethical Relativism** declines to label certain actions as right or wrong. Ethical relativism suggests that what is considered wrong for one person within a certain culture might not be viewed as wrong by someone from a different culture. A behavior deemed unacceptable in one cultural context could be entirely acceptable in another.

THE DECISION

Zayston was an active member of the community in this land but he stayed away from his people for many years when he met his lovely wife. No one knew for sure if his absence was directly linked to his new marriage, but he did stop attending events and giving support to others' events when his wife came into his life. Because they wanted to exist in their own corners, they would handle their own tragedy themselves when it came. It is sometimes said that happy people can be selfish. This is because they do not care about any other thing when they are happy. When people are happy, they really do not care how the world feels around them. Was Zayston really happy when his wife came into his life? Is this why he abandoned his people and community? Should the community people raise money in support of his situation?

Zayston's mistake did not mean he would simply be abandoned by his people in such a situation or condition. It was too harsh of a punishment. After discussing with several individuals, the young president made the final decision. The people were to raise money and support Zayston. Besides this decision, many individuals in the community were heartbroken and simply felt compelled to support Zayston. He was a nice guy, and many men and women genuinely liked him. Both women and men teamed up to launch a massive fund-raiser. The women organized home and hospital visiting hours to support his family interchangeably. Some volunteered to babysit his children, while others volunteered to take them back and forth from school. The men and women did everything they could to help Zayston's wife concentrate on him and the illness he was fighting.

Zayston himself was very mentally strong. His leukemia diagnosis did not affect him mentally. Those who visited him in the hospital said that his body was depreciating, but his mind was very alert and oriented to person, place, and time. Many people were bamboozled by his mental state. He made jokes, he laughed at jokes, and he smiled when he needed to. His conversations were still reasonable and easy to follow. He had fortitude[45]. Conclusively, Zayston never sounded like someone with a serious terminal illness undergoing chemotherapy.

Chemotherapy drugs are hard on the body. This is because they destroy not only cancer cells but also normal healthy cells. This is part of the cause of the enormous side effects that come with chemotherapy treatments. Patients lose appetite, their immune systems become weaker, and they develop

---

[45]Fortitude; strength of mind that enables a person to encounter danger or bear pain or adversity with courage. Definition of fortitude by Merrian-Webser Dictionary.

alopecia[46]. Alopecia is usually seen in cancer patients undergoing chemotherapy treatments. Another symptom associated with Chemotherapy is **Cachexia**[47]. This causes extreme weight loss and muscle wasting. It is a symptom of numerous chronic conditions, including cancer, chronic renal failure, HIV, and multiple sclerosis. According to researchers at Johns Hopkins University, cancer is the second leading cause of death in the United States. The first leading cause of death is heart disease, the second is cancer, and the third is *medical errors*. The general growing belief is that cancer is more deadly nowadays than AIDS. My mother once told me she prefers AIDS to cancer. I responded to her, "Mom, I don't want you to have any." However, there is some truth to what she said. Nowadays, there are many antiviral drugs you can take and live a normal life for decades if you are diagnosed with HIV. On the other hand, when diagnosed with cancer, the disease and the treatment seemed to take away life faster. Do not get me wrong, there are cancer survivors out there – many! Thousands of cancer survivors have undergone chemotherapy treatments, and they are

---

[46]Alopecia is the partial or complete loss of hair from the areas of the body where it normally grows. It's usually seen with cancer patients undergoing chemotherapy treatment.

47Cachexia is a condition that causes extreme weight loss and muscle wasting. It is a symptom of many chronic conditions, such as cancer, chronic renal failure, HIV, and multiple sclerosis.

doing just fine in life. If cancer is diagnosed early enough, the patient has a greater chance of surviving.

The community's decision to help support their brother, Zayston, was made on moral grounds. Compassion is greater than vengeance. This is how the people saw it. Only after the people have helped their brother Zayston, one of their own wills are will they be qualified to be in a position to explain to him the benefit of working as a group or a community. Individuals have to show compassion and help their fellow individuals first before they can have any moral authority to educate them about participating in their survival. *"If we don't learn to share when we don't have, we may never share even when we have."* *This phrase is credited to **Tapang Ivo Tanka.** *[48]

Cheated Death

Zayston and his wife appreciated the president and the entire community. The help was enormous to them. In fact, it was a light bulb in their lives. It made them see *a light of good* in the community. Zayston was a man of fortitude, but the support he got fortified him even further. Miraculously, he recovered from his illness and walked out of that hospital. He even went back to his job at a Nursing Rehab Center. He gained weight, too, and became the normal muscular guy the ladies used to admire. He was so strong that he went back to play soccer,

---

[48]Tapang Ivo Tanku is an activist for the liberation struggle of the newest unrecognized country.

football, and other physical contact sports he enjoyed. The entire community was flabbergasted by his recovery, although they were very, very happy. That is, Zayston made the people in the community very happy with his recovery. Many people developed hope and inspiration from his story. Due to his miraculous recovery, some said, "The Community Cheated Death."

Ambazonian Medical Center and the doctors who treated him used his story to publicize their efforts at good medicine. His recovery gave hope not only to the community but also to many cancer patients across the city. The news was everywhere, including the TV. It spread like wildfire!

Chapter 17 - Stabbed in the Heart

The success of Zayston's medical recovery brought a lot of joy to the hearts of many people in the community and the entire city. Like most people, the young president also visited Mr. Zayston's home after his recovery. He went to visit him with his mother. "Thank you, Mr. Zayston, for not stabbing our hearts," the president once told him. "Your recovery brought a lot of relief to the minds of our people. Thank you for fighting CANCER the way you did."

Personally, I think Zayston should be used as a coach to other patients. He remained remarkably positive throughout his illness, never thinking or speaking like someone facing a life-threatening condition. As mentioned earlier, the city hospital shared his story to inspire hope in others battling similar illnesses. The community jubilated over his recovery, and there was great relief and excitement. However, the people were not ready for the real tragedy to come. This time, the community was stabbed in the heart. Zayston's problem was a simple brush of wings of death. This time, the community could not cheat death. It was stabbed in the heart with what happened next.

Was Zayston's survival a warning sign to the people? How could it have been interpreted? There were no warning signs as to what happened next.

There was no obvious illness, and there were no clues.

Continue to read below. READ, READ, READ…!!!

Someone in the community died! It was sudden. The president got a call at approximately 11:30 pm on that Monday night. The president was seated in his bedroom, reading a book, when his phone rang. He thought of ignoring the call. When he glanced at the caller ID screen, he noticed that it was Mr. Beebong. Mr. Beebong is one person who did not call the president for no reason. Everyone around understood that Mr. Beebong did not call the president without a reason. The young president picked up the phone.

President; "Yes, Mr. Beebong,"

Mr. Beebong; "President, what are you doing? Are you asleep?"

President; "No, I happened to be up late reading."

Mr. Beebong; "Have you heard the news?"

President; "What news?"

Mr. Beebong; "ChengLee is dead,"

The president was in total shock. His heart rate pounded about 130 beats per minute. The normal adult heart rate [49]beats 60 to 100 beats per minute, but he was beating at 130.

President; "What? What happened? Where is his body?"

Mr. Beebong; "He has been taken to the Immanuel Medical Center. His body is still in the Emergency Room."

The president was in total shock. His heart rate pounded about 130 beats per minute at rest. The normal adult heartbeat is 60 to 100 beats per minute, but his was beating at 130 per minute.

Usually, few things came to this young president as a surprise. Those who knew him understood that he could be very tough no matter the situation. But this death took him by surprise. Immediately getting the news, he got up and threw the book he was reading on the wall. After doing that, he took a deep breath and tried to compose himself. There was a 50 by 30-inch mirror on the wall in his room. He gazed into the mirror for 10 minutes without moving any voluntary muscles. The sclera of his eyes became red and then watery. But there was no time for tears. He turned around and went to the wardrobe. It was summertime. He put on some tennis shoes, a jean trousers, and a white T-shirt. The president walked

---

[49]The normal adult heart beats 60 to 100 beats per minute. Infant Heart Rate is 100 to 160 beats per minute. Infants have faster heartbeats than adults because their body is still developing and so they need a lot of oxygen from blood to nourish and develop their organ

out of his room and into the living room. His roommate sat on the couch in the living room, drinking a Budweiser beer while watching a video on his phone.

Roommate; "You look so distressed, Mr. President, what is it?"

He asked in a bewildering manner. The president turned, looked at him, and then smiled. The young president did not respond to his question immediately. Instead, he took his phone out of his pocket and opened a video. In that video was ChengLee. The video was sent to the president in a WhatsApp group message by another friend. A friend had forwarded a video of ChengLee himself the day before he died. It was a video of Cheng Lee ChengLee skillfully kicking a soccer ball. In the video, the ball was bouncing on ChengLee's knees and feet, continuously. The video was fun and fun to watch. While ChengLee was kicking the ball in the air, he eventually lost control of it and fell to the ground. There was laughter in the background in the video. His friends who watched him were laughing at him for losing control and falling to the ground. The video was delightful and very funny to watch. The president pulled up the video and walked to his roommate sitting on the couch in the living room. The roommate asked again disturbingly, "Tell me, President, what's going on?"

Roommate; "You look so distressed, Mr. President, what is it?"

117

He asked in a bewildering manner. The young president did not respond to this question immediately. Instead, he took his phone out of his pocket and walked to his roommate sitting on the couch in the living room. He unlocked the phone, opened the 30-second video of ChengLee that was described earlier, and showed the roommate. The video was always delightful and very funny to watch. It was hysterical. The president's roommate burst into laughter while watching the video. The roommate said, "Yes, yes, I know this guy. He is a very cool guy. I saw him yesterday Sunday in the field. He invited me somewhere next week. When I see him next time, I will ask him about it…etc."

The roommate told the president that when he sees ChengLee next time, he will ask ChengLee about something they talked about the last time they met. But the president interrupted the roommate. "No, there will be no next time," he said.

The young president said, "No, there will be no next time."

Roommate; "Why? What do you mean?" He was bewildered, perplexed, and dumbfounded. With a disturbed tone of voice, the roommate asked again, "Tell me, Mr. President, what's going on?"

The young president, "Cyprian Shila, he is dead."

The president told the roommate that ChengLee was dead and there would be no next time to see him.

The young president said, "I'm sorry, Cyprian, he is gone. I got a call approximately fifteen minutes ago that he is dead. There will be no next time. I am on my way to the hospital now where his corpse is."

Cyprian, the roommate, was heartbroken. The president asked if Cyprian wanted to come along with the president to the emergency room to see ChengLee's corpse. He declined. Cyprian was a tough guy, but he knew very little about how to deal with certain tragedies. He could not deal with tragedies well. He was so sad that the president felt some guilt informing him of what had happened. Out to the main living room door, the president left the house. Cyprian remained sad on the red couch for the entire night.

ChengLee's death took the community that evening by shock. The people were shocked, surprised, bewildered, flabbergasted, dumbfounded, bamboozled, aghast and perplexed. The pain cut through everyone's heart like a sharp sword. ChengLee was in a community gathering just the day before he died. He was cracking jokes and having a good time with many friends in the community the day before he died. He appeared to be in good physical health with no noticeable signs or symptoms of illness.

How He Died

ChengLee and his wife were in their living room the night he died. He was holding his phone. Suddenly, his hands and entire body got numbed. He fell on the floor headfirst. His wife was by his side when it all happened. She was frightened. She rushed to lift him off the floor as he dropped, but she was powerless. While on the floor, ChengLee was unresponsive to any verbal or pain stimuli. "Baby, what is it? Wake up, wake up...etc.," she yelled in confusion countless times. His wife called emergency help. The paramedics arrived, dashing onto the third floor of the apartment where they lived. ChengLee was rushed to the hospital, but he never made it. He died on the way. The paramedics did a Cardiopulmonary Resuscitation (CPR). They tried to intubate him, also, but it did not help. The guy was gone; it was too late!

Ambazonia (Southern Cameroon) is the English-speaking region of Cameroon, Africa, which declared its independence in 2017 from The Republic of Cameroon. The Independent liberation movement of Ambazonia is said to have started in September 2016. Other activists in this liberation movement include Eric Tataw, Mark Bareta, Joshua Carr, Yannic Sicot, Akoson Pauline Diale, Cucu Da Blinkz...etc.

The normal adult heart beats 60 to 100 beats per minute. Infant Heart Rate is 100 to 160 beats per minute. Infants have faster heartbeats than adults because their body is still developing and so they need a lot of oxygen from blood to nourish and develop their organ

Chapter 18 - Death in AmbaLand

When the President arrived at the emergency room, it was already crowded with other community members who had heard the news. ChengLee's lifeless body was lying on a gurney in a supine position. The intubation tubes used to open his airway were sticking out of his mouth. His wife was by his bedside with other male and female friends from the community. The room was very quiet. You could hear the sound of someone dropping a needle on the floor. The word to describe the atmosphere was *dead silence*. Everyone's eye appeared swollen from prolonged crying. It was clear or assumed that their tear glands had produced tears to the max. It was a very sad place to be. It even got sadder when you looked at ChengLee's wife. You could not help yourself not to like her. She was a very humble and likable person. Naturally, we are drawn to humility. Our human nature loves humble people. She was humble, and she got along with almost everyone in this community. For such a thing to happen to her was really heartbroken. Moments like this are when people question God. Many people have asked why God allows good people to die suddenly. However, this is the fate of everyone. Good or bad, death is inevitable, and it will come to those we love, those we care for, and those we hate. *Every life ends, but people will always live*. Nature has its own way of clinging to life and it has its own way of getting rid of life for the next generation. In other words, it has its own way of making space for the next generation.

ChengLee's death was sudden, surprising, and difficult for many people in the community. Nevertheless, the young president was able to deal with it. There are specific ways to deal with one's own death and the death of others. Some of these methods are evidence-based research solutions. One way to effectively deal with the death of others is to deal with your own death. One way to deal with your own death is to write about your own death. For example, write a one to two-page paragraph essay of your own death. What would you want your family to say about you? What would you want your family to write on your tombstone? What do you want to be written on your tomb? What do you want others to say about you when you are gone? What would you like to be remembered for? Writing and answering these questions may help you deal with your own death. This is how the young president dealt with ChengLee's death. Many people did not know that he had a deeper understanding of these things. He had graduated from nursing school one year earlier, where he studied Death and Dying during his training. Moreso, he had lost close family members before. The pain of dead and dying was not all too new to him.

Rodriguez Wakanda was one of those who were in the emergency room near ChengLee's lifeless body. He worked with ChengLee in running a medical health business. Like most people, he was a good friend to ChengLee and very attached to him. He stood by ChengLee's corpse for a full hour without blinking. Yes, he did not blink his eyes! You could poke him with a needle, and he would not have felt the pain.

By hospital policy, the emergency room allowed families to stay with a newly deceased body for a specific time limit. This is specifically for the first eight hours of death. The family and many community members had been with ChengLee's corpse for over four hours. The intubation tubes were still in his mouth. Over forty individuals from the community had come in and out of that room. The emergency room nurses were feeling the clustering of people but they could not interrupt. Some say that is why they could not come into the room and take out the intubating tube that was sticking out from ChengLee's mouth.

Nurses and medical professionals sometimes face difficulties taking corpses from family members, especially after a sudden death. I recall a story from one nurse. She mentioned a woman in her forties who died from liver cancer. The pain had been so severe that her husband could barely touch her. After she passed away, he climbed into the hospital bed and held her body for hours. There was no way any medical staff could go in and drag him away from her to remove the woman's corpse. The husband was on his deceased wife's body for over four hours.

The staff allowed him to take as long as he needed to be close to her one last time. This was what was happening in this emergency room that day with ChengLee. His wife was holding his corpse, and it was difficult to get her off it. She was saying her goodbyes.

ChengLee's corpse was taken to the mortuary after the permission of his wife, who was the surrogate and *Power of Attorney*. A power of attorney has the authority to act on behalf of another person when that person is no longer capable of deciding. Here, ChengLee's wife was his power of attorney and next of kin. It is important to note that being married to someone does not automatically make you their power of attorney. You do not need to be married to someone to become their power of attorney, either. And you do not become someone's power of attorney because you are married to them. A power of attorney is usually chosen by the person himself when he or she is alive and capable of making their own decisions. He or she can choose someone he or she is married to. He or she can also choose someone he or she is not married to. One only becomes the power of attorney if chosen by the patient when the patient is alive and capable of deciding. You do not become a person's power of attorney simply because you are married to them. Nevertheless, in a case without power of attorney, *Health Law* automatically assigns the spouse to become the power of attorney.

ChengLee's wife was chosen by ChengLee to be his power of attorney. She gave the order for the body to be taken to the mortuary after everyone was prepared to leave the emergency room. That was around four in the morning. They were all exhausted from crying.

Funeral Procession

ChengLee was given a good funeral procession. There was a lot of support from the community to his family. His sisters and friends from around the world flew into the country to attend his funeral. A massive contribution was made to aid the funeral expenditures. There were rumors and dilemmas between his wife and his family on who had full control of his corpse, property, and businesses. ChengLee's family is said to have a lot of influence on him and his siblings. He came from a family of about 8 siblings. His family was rigid and controlled a lot of things about their lives. They were from a very strict religious background. However, it was known to the community that ChengLee was an independent thinker. He was a man with his own mind, and his family had a difficult time influencing his decisions. We do not know if his wife and 3-year-old son inherited most of what he had, but they eventually came home successfully after the burial. His body was taken about 5000 miles away from his homeland.

His corpse was taken away to his homeland.

Disclosure

ChengLee was a heavy smoker. He smoked a lot and drank alcohol regularly. This can cause **atherosclerosis**[50], which is a disease. It was said that ChengLee's cardiac doctor had instructed him several times to quit smoking and drinking. It is believed that he died of a heart attack. There was also news of negligence from his cardiac doctor. The doctor had failed to address several of his complaints in his follow up appointments. In the week of his passing, some claimed he had visited the doctor with specific symptoms that needed attention, but no action was taken.

---

[50]Atherosclerosis is a disease of the circulatory system of the body. It is the hardening and narrowing of the arteries in the blood vessels of the body. Atherosclerosis leads to high blood pressure and eventually heart attack if it is not controlled. As we age, it slowly, quietly, gradually, and silently blocks arteries in the body. Alcohol, cigarette smoking, and a sedentary lifestyle a high-risk factor for developing atherosclerosis.

Who or what killed ChengLee? Sarcastically, he often expressed that he would never go back to his homeland. He joked that only his corpse would return to his homeland. *The tongue is very powerful. Many times, what we say manifests itself.* Again, what killed ChengLee? Was it the power of his tongue? Was it the doctor's negligence? Was it the heart attack that killed him? Was it his lovely wife? What did the police report say about his death? Was it atherosclerosis? No one knows the answer to these questions. It is open for your own brainstorming.

The community was in agony due to ChengLee's death, but his wife was more agonized than anyone else. For many months, she grieved. Like I said, she was a very calm, quiet, and humble woman who never bothered anyone. Nevertheless, it was reasonable by law to question her about her husband's death. Legally, when an unexpected death occurs in a house, everyone in that house becomes a suspect until the police prove otherwise. Legally, she was seen as a suspect to her husband's death. It was sad to know that she had to be screened for any suspicious activity surrounding her husband's death. But it had to be done based on the law of the land. It is worth understanding that *no one* is incapable of committing murder. That is, everyone is capable of committing murder. It does not matter how nice, quiet, humble, religious, or peace-loving a person is; he or she is still capable of committing murder. The point is that people just have different *motives*. This is why the police do not exclude suspecting anyone under such circumstances. Some people will take away life for 10,000 USD, others will only do so if the money is 1 million USD and above, and others will take away someone's life if only the money is greater than 100 million USD. Some people will never kill anyone for any amount of money, but if you abuse their children, they will do just that. More so, some people will never take away a life for money, and they will never take away someone's life, even if their children are abused. However, this same person will take away your life if you stand in a position to damage their reputation or political career. Some people will murder if their wife or husband has sex with someone else. It does not matter how nice, calm, good, and religious they are; they will commit murder if their spouse cheats on them. Even the Holy Roman Catholic Pope is capable of committing murder. What will cause a pope to do such a horrible thing? Can you come up with a motive or scenario that may compel the Pope, the Holy Father, to commit murder? Remember that priests and high priests murdered Jesus. These were good, extremely religious men who had *motives* to kill him. With a motive at heart, they forgot all their good religious principles and murdered Jesus, the savior.

The above lengthy explanation boils down to one thing. I am practically trying to understand why ChengLee's wife needed to be interviewed and questioned by the police. A lot of people in the community hated it and could not see why. They could not understand why anyone would look at ChengLee's nice, loving, and humble wife from such a perspective. It was not right, given who she was. On the other hand, it was not an incorrect thing to see her like a suspect who needed to be interviewed. It was a proper thing according to the legality of the situation in this foreign land. She was a good woman and nothing suspicious was uncovered about her. Like most members of the community, she was a victim of this loss. Like most members, she remained mourning her husband's death for a long time.

Chapter 19 - The Moral of the Story

Many people want to succeed in life, but usually, they are not willing to receive the baggage success brings. To an extent, we are all guilty of this. Great wealth comes with great responsibilities; great powers come with great responsibilities. Responsibilities are the baggage of success. The more success we achieve in life, the more people look up to us for their responsibilities. More so, the more successful you get in life, the more envy and jealousy that may come your way. "The more money we come across is like the more problems we see," The Notorious B.I.G.[51] from Brooklyn, New York, once said in his hit song. The title of that song is "Mo Money, Mo Problems" by The Notorious B.I.G.[52]

"The more money we come across is like the more problems we see."

The Notorious B.I.G

Do you want to be successful? Are you willing to accept the responsibilities and obligations that come with success? Should people quit striving for a successful life because of these expected pressures? How did this young president deal with his own success? What would you learn after reading the paragraphs below?

---

[52] B.I.G; Business Instead of Games

Where attention goes, energy flows. The attention of the community was on ChengLee's death. He was one of the president's top key allies and advisors. Generally, his ideas focused on modesty. He contributed to the president's success by reminding him how important it is to be humble and modest. The grandiose personality of the president sometimes hindered him from appearing modest. ChengLee saw that, and he tried to make a difference. He was not the type of person who would see your fault and then talk behind your back. He tried to be sincere and respectful. He understood constructive criticism.[53].

Before ChengLee died, there had been varying ongoing tensions in the community group. His death dissolved many of the tensions that were growing. It soaked the energy away from the problems. Some of it was around the young president's success. ChengLee's death diverted the attention, the envies, and the gloating away from the president.

A lot of progress was made before ChengLee died. The young president led the organization, organized his people, and improved communications greatly. The young president and his team established massive communication methods that moved people

---

[53]**Constructive Criticism;** the process of offering well valid opinion with the intent to improve the person being criticized instead of harm. It usually involves both positive and negative comments in a friendly manner rather than an oppositional one. *Source*; https://www.definitions.net

from one end of the city to the other. The people became more organized and cooperative with their community activities. The community had records of everyone's contact information and many other complex personal data. The president developed a census plan to carry out statistics on the number of individuals in the community. This had *never* been done before. Names, ages, heights, professional careers, number of children, and other statistics were all collected by this president. It is worth noting that you can never effectively manage a group, a community, or a country without statistics. Usually, leaders make effective decisions about people based on their knowledge of the statistics of the people. The young president understood the importance of this. He took statistics of everything he could and then used them in successful decision-making processes. It was a successful strategic reform.

But the successes this young man experienced did not come without a price. That is, his success did not come on a platter of gold. He lost a lot of friends and made many new enemies for trying to do the right thing. There is a saying that; "If you are a leader and everyone likes you, chances are, you are not doing your job well." This is how the young man made many enemies because of his leadership. Like other successes in life, his success sparked some real envy and jealousy in some individuals in that community. As he grew in power, his job became a source of prestige instead of a source of responsibility, especially in the eyes of the envious ones. In the eyes of some elites in that community, he was seen as a rising, powerful young man instead of a young man with the weight of responsibility of his people. When he took over the responsibility of being the president, no one wanted the position. In fact, it was a *laughable matter*. The young man worked hard and restructured the entire community and its organization. He took the little or nothing that was given to him and made the best out of it. As time went on, his fame and attention grew. As a result, some individuals became envious of the fame, attention, and respect he was receiving.

Chapter 20 - The Plot and the Night of Reckoning

In this small community, the Young President had once been a beacon of hope. Elected on a platform of unity and progress, he promised to bring prosperity to the community. His infectious charisma and speeches excited the hearts of many. But as the days, weeks, months, and years rolled on, the very people who had once rallied behind him began to feel a twinge of unease. But how? When? How did it happen?

The President's popularity soared, and with it, his power. He introduced sweeping reforms that transformed the community into a bustling hub of activities. New members and businesses moved into the community. Both businesses and new members of the community organization flourished, and the town's once-quiet streets buzzed with life. From children to adolescents, from adolescents to adults, from adults to older adults, and from older adults to seniors, everyone was happy with the president's swiping transforming reforms. However, as the President basked in the glow of his success, a dark cloud began to gather over the town. Who were these dark clouds? Where were they? How did it unfold?

It started with whispers in the shadows at a local bar. A group of the president's former supporters, including advisors, now feeling overshadowed by his brilliance and popularity, began to gather in the dimly lit corners of the local bars. They called themselves the *Discontented Coalition*. Among them was Rodriguez Wakanda, a once-ambitious entrepreneur whose bakery had been eclipsed by the president's new food market growth initiative. He could not keep up with the competition of the growth of new bakeries. As such, he lost a lot of revenue. Rodriguez Wakanda blamed the president for his loss. He was a grumpy fellow who had also lost his position as the town's unofficial historian and intellectual. Countless times, he had lost poignant and vital intellectual debates against the president. Some of it were in the community's public square with many people in the community listening. Because of the young President, he could no longer command the attention he once enjoyed at community events.

"Can you believe it?" Rodriguez Wakanda scoffed as his hands flourished dramatically.

"He's taken everything from us! We need to do something before he becomes a dictator!" Miss Defao grunted in agreement.

"A dictator, indeed! We should remove him from power. He's become too strong, too popular. It's time we remind him who really runs this community!" Said Miss Defao.

"What if we... I don't know, make him disappear? Just for a little while? A little scare to knock him down a peg?" Mr. Beebong mischievously expressed while leaning in closer to the deadly circle they had formed.

Mr. Beebong, Miss Defao, and Rodriguez Wakanda were at a local bar brainstorming and spearheading the plot and night of reckoning against the president. There were many others involved but these were the masterminds behind the plot. The trio exchanged conspiratorial glances, and their minds raced with mischievous possibilities of ways to make the president disappear. In the dark corner of the local bar and under that moonlight night, the supposed deadly plan was born. They would gather the community folks who felt similarly betrayed and orchestrate a coup against their once-beloved president. They were ready for any outcome, including his death.

As the days passed, the *Discontented Coalition* grew bolder. They rallied members of the community group, townspeople, and street corners. They started injecting spinning tales of the president's supposed tyranny and greed. "He's hoarding all the glory for himself!" they shouted and cried out loud in private gatherings. "We deserve our share!" The townsfolk, fueled by a mix of nostalgia and resentment, began to chant for the president's downfall.

Meanwhile, the Young President remained blissfully and unaware of the spinning tales and storm that was building against him. He was busy planning the annual Community Festival, a celebration meant to honor the community's achievements. Little did he know, the very people he sought to uplift were plotting his demise.

The night of the festival arrived. It was the night of reckoning, according to the plotters. The community square was alive with laughter and music. Colorful banners fluttered in the breeze, and the scent of roasted meats, hotdogs, and other foods filled the air of the streets and the balconies of the homes nearby. The president, dressed in his finest suit, took to the stage, ready to deliver a speech that would inspire hope and further unity. Everyone had gathered around the podium where he was to make his speech. Some people stood on the balcony of their homes near the crowded streets. The atmosphere was enthusiastic and blissful.

As the young president began to speak, the *Discontented Coalition* emerged from the shadows of the homes near the street. They emerged behind the backyard of the compound, brandishing torches and pitchforks. "Nonsenses, damn with you, Mr. President!" they shouted. One could hear their voices, a cacophony of anger and betrayal. Upon looking at their faces, the young president was shocked to see the hatred, vexation, and willingness to do harm against him. They approached the stage shouting from three angles: left, right, and in front of the president. As they matched towards the stage, their conspirators joined them and moved towards the president as to grab him. The president's heart raced as he realized the gravity of the situation. "Wait! We can talk about this!" he pleaded, but the crowd was deafened by their own fury, envy, hatred, and vice that had been injected into their minds by the *Discontented Coalition*. They were destined to do harm. While this was happening, supporters of the president curved in, too. Together, they started matching around him to form a circle of protective barriers. The atmosphere was tense, and people started swigging punches. Some fell to the floor, and others ramble over them. Two minutes into the chaos, there were loud sounds; "Bang, bang, bang, bang… etc." Gunshots were heard all over the air. No one knew where the shots were coming from but it made the chaos even worse. People ran and scattered in all directions. Some were running towards the 'bang noise'; others were running in the opposite direction. Some dove to the floor! It was frightening and chaotic.

Two Minutes and The Great Escape

Just as the mob surged forward, a strange twist of fate intervened. This was two minutes as the chaos exploded. Mr. Beebong, Rodriguez and Miss Defao were running towards the podium to the president from three directions. They got caught up in their own fervor and accidentally tripped over each other sending them tumbling in front of the podium. They had emerged from three opposite directions but collided at the center where there was distance between the president and the crowd. The chaos that ensued was both terrifying and comical as townsfolk stumbled over one another, trying to avoid the flailing limbs of the Coalition.

Lady Ness and some other members were extraordinary die-hard supporters of the president. They screamed and shouted as loud as their lungs could. This was what raised everyone's awareness that the approach of the trio, *Discontented Coalition*, towards the stage was not some prank. It had first appeared like a prank since one of these individuals was known to be an advisor to the president. But on this day of reckoning, Mr. Beebong was not here to give any advice. He was running towards the podium to harm the young president just like the other two members of the coalition. As Lady Ness and others screamed at the top of their lungs, it became clear there was danger.

In the midst of the pandemonium, the young president spotted a narrow alleyway behind the stage in the backyard. He broke through the protective circle that was being formed around him. With a burst of adrenaline, he dashed towards it, narrowly avoiding the grasp of the angry mob. He ran through the alley, his heart pounding, until he found himself in a hidden garden, overgrown and wild. He lay flat on the ground for two minutes, trying to escape a suspicious person he himself did not trust. He controlled his breathing so as not to create any further noise at his hiding spot. Within two minutes, after that suspect had walked away, he stood up, running again in a safer direction.

As the president caught his breath, he realized he was almost killed. While still making sense of the situation, he was met by an unexpected sight: a group of children playing. Their laughers were ringing like bells of freedom to his ear. He jerked backward in fear and then realized it was the noise of children. They were oblivious to the chaos happening several blocks away and lost in their own world of imagination. In that moment, the young president realized that his true power lay not in his popularity or influence but in the joy and hope he could inspire in others. He saw the joy in the children's faces as they played. He saw how pure and innocent they carried themselves while playing. There is no telling what happened to this president when he saw those children but we know for sure he changed his mind when meeting them.

With renewed determination, he decided to confront the *Discontented Coalition* not with anger but with understanding and innocent. He returned to the festival, where the mob was still in disarray, and called out to them from a safe position. It was a dangerous move, but he felt inspired to do it. The young president managed to pass through and go to a safe angle on the podium. The crowd, still simmering with anger, paused to listen. They were also flabbergasted to see him on that stage. The few people who wanted the day to be bloody had been subdued by the community crowd itself. Some of their hands were physically tied from ropes people made from thorn pieces of their clothing.

"Friends! I see your pain, your frustration but let's not tear each other apart. Together, we can find a way to share this glory!" The president started blasting words to the crowd with the same megaphone he had dropped when escaping the stage. He went on for about 30 minutes with a brilliant speech. He spoke about the history of the community and how far they have come to be in such a situation. He also spoke of the challenges of the day, the death of ChengLee, the economic situation of the community members, and the way forward to *Love, Peace,* and *Unity*.

The president's sincerity cut through the tense crowd like a knife. It was what the members and townspeople really needed to hear. Slowly, the members of the community who wanted to harm him began to lower their torches, pitchforks, knives, and even guns. Like day and night, their expressions shifted from rage to contemplation. The young man was charismatic and, on this day, it served him and his people well.

Mr. Beebong, Rodriguez, and Miss Defao, still tangled in their own mists, looked up sheepishly. "Maybe we got a little carried away," Miss Defao admitted, her cheeks flushed. She looked humiliated.

The president smiled, extending a hand to help them up. "Let's work together to ensure everyone in this community and its association feels valued. We can create a community where no one feels overshadowed." There was a great relief from the crowd and a roar of applauded. The majority of the guests wanted peace and good times. As the festival resumed, laughter and music filled the air once more. The *Discontented Coalition,* now transformed into a group of allies, joined the president on stage, ready to forge a new path together. The night ended not with a coup or bloodshed but with a celebration of unity. This proved that even in the face of betrayal, chaos, or war, hope could still prevail. No one knew how it happened, but it was done! The president did it! The community learned that true strength lies not in power but in the bonds of community, laughter, and the occasional mishap that brings everyone together.

Making Sense of Love, Envy, Hatred, and Jealousy

We often preach or talk about LOVE.[54]. It is an emotion that we are familiar with. It is arguably the best emotion we can ever experience in life, though

---

[54]Love is an emotion we are much familiar with. The word *LOVE* has many meanings and many definitions to many different people. But in this context, we are talking of LOVE as an emotion.

it is not the highest *positive emotion.*[55] of the human *Emotion Frequency Vibrational Scale.* More so, the same word can mean something for someone but has a completely different meaning for another person. This is why we must be clear in communicating with others or ourselves! There are endless and different ways we use or express the word *love*. Examples of such expressions;

1. "I love you, Mimi."

2. "She loves that chair."

3. "Such a loving God"

4. "You love your life"

5. "I want to make love"

6. "I love Pascal Presentations LLC"

7. "........................."

---

[55] The word Emotion in metaphysics means; Energy in Motion (E-Motion). The human body vibrates in particular motions. Some are positive and others are negative. Shame, Anger, Guild, Grief are all negative emotions of the human body. They are at the bottom of the Vibrational Frequency Emotional Chart. Love, Joy, Peace, Enlightenment are positive emptions and are at the top section of the chart.

We often preach or talk about Love. It is arguably the best emotion we can ever experience.

Because we are familiar with love, it is sometimes easy for us to know how to deal with this emotion. But there are other intangible things or emotions in us we do not give familiarity to. We do not train ourselves, our children and our communities how to manage and deal with some of these emotions. For example, *hatred, envy,* and *jealousy.* These emotions were present in this community. Just like love, *hatred, envy,* and *Jealousy* are feelings and emotions all humans experience. The challenge is to suppress these types of feelings and emotions to prevent yourself from ever taking control of yourself. *Hatred, envy,* and *jealousy* are negative emotions on the *Emotion Frequency Vibrational Scale.* The purpose of these emotions or feelings is to compel or motivate humanity to navigate circumstances. Even God in heaven is an envious and jealous God.

Hatred, *jealousy*, and *envy* are emotions that are as old as humanity itself. A good example of the manifestation of these emotions is seen in the biblical story of David, the shepherd boy, and Saul, the King of Israel at the time. When Saul became the first King of Israel, the bible noted there was joy. The Bible described Saul as a wise, tall, and handsome man. He was the people of Israel's choice for king. The Bible said that the people of Israel wanted a king. For a long time, after the freedom from slavery in Egypt, the people of Israel were ruled by prophets, judges, priests, and high priests. At some point, they pressured the prophet Samuel that they wanted a king to be their ruler. Every neighboring country around them had kings, so they wanted a king, too. The people of Israel wanted a king ruler just like their neighboring kingdoms. As such, King Saul became the first king of Israel.

After David killed Goliath, King Saul put David in charge of his army. David won many battles, and he became very popular. Whenever David came home from war, the women would come out dancing and singing, "Saul has struck down thousands, and David has struck down tens of thousands!" The women did this as a sign of praise and measure, but to King Saul, it was disrespectful to his ego. Saul became jealous of these chants. He did not like it but had no way of stopping the people from chanting that without revealing his inner *Jealous* feelings. Saul became so *envious* and *jealous* of David that he wanted him dead. The key word here is *Jealous*.

Again, this emotion is as old as humanity itself. Saul became so *envious* of David that his *envy, jealousy,* and *hatred* became uncontrollable.

Saul's first son was called Jonathan. He wanted his son to be king of Israel after him, but he feared that David would become king someday due to his enormous popularity. Saul became so uncontrollably *jealous* that he plotted and actively tried to kill David. One day, Saul took an army of 3,000 men and went hunting for David. Imagine yourself being searched by 3,000 armed soldiers in the woods. What will you do? Imagine this happening to you due to the *envy, jealousy,* and *hatred* of the president of your nation.

While hunting for David in the woods, bushes, and hills, King Saul got tired and decided to take a rest in a nearby cave. Coincidentally, he entered the very cave where David and his men were hiding. But he did not know that David and his men were hiding inside the same cave. David's men whispered to David, "This is your chance to kill Saul." David heard what they said and then made his move. He crept toward Saul at the back and cut off a piece of his royal robe. David did not kill Saul. He spared his life. King Saul did not notice David, neither did he notice a piece of his royal robe was cut off. David left the cave quietly and did not allow his men to attack Saul and his men.

David left the cave and climbed to a nearby mountain that overlooked Saul's position. He shouted: "Abner, why didn't you protect your king? Where are Saul's jug and spear? This is a piece of his robe I cut while hiding in the cave!" Saul recognized David's voice and was astonished, flabbergasted, bewildered, and dumbfounded. He looked at his robe and saw that David was telling the truth. He and his men were extremely embarrassed. Saul said: "You could have killed me, but you did not. I know that you will be the next king of Israel." Saul left the scene and went back to his palace like a sad puppy. David will not see him again after that. Not long after, King Saul committed suicide in a battle by throwing himself on his own spear. He did not want to be a captive to the enemies they were fighting. His men lost a war and the enemies were closing on to him. To prevent himself from being captured, he threw himself on his sword and died by suicide. His *envy, jealousy,* and *hatred* went to the grave with him.

But not all in Saul's family hated David. King Saul's first son, Jonathan, *loved* David. He protected David often from his father's *envy* and *jealousy.* Many times, he was sharing information with David to protect his life. Several times in the story, he successfully removed David from his father's evil and deadly plots. Saul was unsuccessful in killing David not only because of David's wisdom and bravery but also primarily because of his own son,

Jonathan. Jonathan gave David a lot of intelligence.[56] that helped him escape. When David became the next king of Israel, Jonathan was protected and highly favored.

In the above biblical anecdote, we learn how King Saul's son, Jonathan, protected David from his father's *envy* and *jealousy*. Just as Jonathan protected David from his father's *envy* and *jealousy*, that is how many others in this community protected the president from the *envy* and *jealousy* of other powerful community members. When the young man became president, the original and general prediction was that he was not going to last six months in his position. The majority of the people believed he would be grind, chewed, and spat away by the fury and vicious criticism practices that existed in the community. To everyone's surprise, it was five years, and he was still standing tall as the active president. He will remain president for four years after winning 99% of the community's vote. The young man had a *thick skin.*[57] . Very few things disturbed him. Insults, envy, criticisms, disappointments, betrayals... etc. None of these really

---

[56] Intelligence in this context means "Secrete information." For example; the FBI, CIA, Mossad and other Secret Service intelligence organizations share *intelligence* to capture and neutralize threats.

[57] Thick Skin; the ability to keep from getting upset or offended by the things other people say or to you. For example; President Obama and President Trump have a very thick skin when it comes to criticism.

penetrated him. He had a thick skin. This was one quality that made him successful as a leader. His haters became very frustrated.

Again, envy, *jealousy, and hatred* are feelings all humans experience. The challenge is to suppress it and prevent yourself from ever being blind by it. Like King Saul, some people are so blind and carried away by their envy and sense of jealousy that they forget to realize their own talents and gifts they have. As such, they wander into life, not making use of and multiplying the fruits of their talents. This kind of mindset is a disaster for self-improvement. It is known as *Lack of Mindset*[58].

Just as we suppress and control our feelings of *anger*, we must do everything to suppress and control our feelings of *envy* and *jealousy*. These feelings are not there to hurt us. They are there to help us better ourselves. We can use them to control others or guide others to do the right thing. For example, parents use jealousy to keep their kids in control. Sometimes, kids get jealous when their father or mother gives more attention to the other siblings. In other to win that attention, children will do everything correctly to win their mother or father's attention back from their siblings. The jealousy in them forces them to behave right toward others to get their parent's

---

[58] A person who is too envious and jealous is Living in Lack. That is, he or she does not focus on the good qualities they have. Their focus is on the negative. The opposite of Lack Mindset is Abundance Mindset.

attention. The child horridly succumbs to the request of the parent, thereby being controlled.

Sometimes, wives and husbands use jealousy to make the other partner love them more. There are women who deliberately seek their spouse's attention by making them feel more jealous. They make them feel that she, the wife, is flirting with some other man. I have seen this from my own personal experience. You, reading now, must have also seen it from your own personal experience. The woman gives the spouse the impression that some other man is flirting with her and trying to date her. When the husband notices this, he becomes *jealous* and then desires his wife more. Vice versa, men do the same to their women. All these spark *jealousies,* but the *jealousies* in this content become a type used for bonding.

Jealousy and *envy* sometimes lead to healthy competition. Nations have used *jealousy* as a motivation to improve their people. In the 1950s and 1960s, the United States and the Soviet Union became *envious* and *jealous* of one another so much that they motivated their scientists and citizens to achieve a lot of useful innovations. For example, the Soviet Union and The United States sent a man to the moon within the same time period in history. Both countries also developed nuclear weapons at similar times – the middle of the 20th Century. This was called the Space Race.[59]. These two nations were forced to compete with one another not only because of their safety but also through the trigger of *envy* and *jealousy*. Each country had set out to outsmart the other. Their embassies in both countries were loaded with the world's most sophisticated spy apparatus your mind can imagine at the time. Their *envy* for each other created a competitive path that led to many new technological discoveries.

These are some of the uses of the feelings of *envy* and *jealousy*. They can create room for positive growth in our lives if we truly understand them. They are there to help us grow instead of destroying each other. This was the young president's message to his community in this foreign land. As humans, in other to survive and live a happy life, we need to make a conscious effort to seek the meaning or beauty of all the emotions in us, including negative emotions like *jealousy, envy, hatred, anger, sadness, anxiousness,* and more...etc. Understanding and knowing how to manage these emotions is a true testament to our personal growth and survival, especially in our daily relationships with families, friends, and community.

---

[59] The space race was a **20th Century** struggle between two nation-states, the Soviet Union (USSR) and the United States (US).

The True Moral of the Story

Not sometimes, but often in life, we do not know what we want. Perhaps this is the primary moral of the story of this community. Sometimes, even when we know what we want, our *hatred, envy, jealousy,* and *bigotry* get in the way to prevent us from receiving it. The people wanted a unified community; they wanted their community organization saved from falling apart, and they wanted their community to have a strong, rigid structure. The young president gave them all what they desired but they could not receive it. Their *envy, jealousy, hatred,* and *bigotry* got in the way. They never enjoyed their gift of the young man as much as they could. They never enjoyed the young man's talents and his full potential. It can also be said that *what we wish for does not always make us happy.*

Because of his genuine love and hard work in the community, the young president gained admiration and became very powerful. He also had a lot of support from well-wishers in neighboring communities in this foreign land. The young man had *Power and Control*. This made a lot of elites uncomfortable, especially those who had underestimated him from the beginning. The people were not prepared for this side of the unity they desired. Like King Saul, some individuals and elites who had supported the president became *envious* and *jealous.* They could not absorb the respect and attention he was receiving. In life, some people will support you as long as you are beneath them. As soon as you start achieving and rising above them, they start to dislike you. This is some of the price associated with success and we all must be ready for it. There were many individuals in the community who were not willing to pay the price of what they were seeking. Some allowed their *envy* and *jealousy* to control them to turn against the president. There was so much animosity. People found fault in everything that did not matter. Things got worse. The relationship became a *cat-and-mouse game* because the young president also did not back down on the attacks against him. To him, there were cheap attacks that needed to be addressed. However, it became overwhelming and personal.

Another moral of this story is that an entire society may go astray when good people keep quiet. If the good people do not stand up against the hateful ones, society will be penetrated by hate and eventually go astray from everyone's liking. Lady Ness was a courageous and good woman who made it a habit to stand up against hatred. She did not do it only for the president, but she stood up for other people, too. Through her presence, a lot of negativities were neutralized in several community gatherings thereby keeping the peace and unity.

Disclosing The Despondent

The despondency[60] and decline the community once experienced came as a result of many things. It is worth disclosing that this young president was sometimes hard in his final decisions against individual members. Sometimes, he did not listen to the opinions of some of the elites. Though his reasons for this were reasonable, the act made some people feel alienated. Generally, everyone in a group wants to feel that their voice is being heard. When individuals start to feel their voices and opinions are not being considered, they start becoming resistant to ideas, change and growth. In a community of people, everybody counts. It does not matter how insignificant the person may appear; everybody counts. As an ordinary person, this may not matter, but when in a leadership role, it does matter a lot. Everybody's ideas must be taken into consideration, no matter how dumb and backward they sound. It was a moral and leadership lesson the young president learned the hard way.

Like most successful young men, the young man's success did get into his head sometimes. He became boastful of some of his accomplishments. Sometimes, he did it appropriately, and other times, he did it inappropriately. Those looking for faults

---

[60] Despondent; in low spirits from loss of hope or courage.

"She grew more and more despondent." Definition from Oxford Dictionary Languages.

were quick to pick on it. They gave him hard times and then used it as talking points to interrupt his popularity. The moral of this part is that *be humble no matter how successful you are*. If you are too proud of your accomplishments, it can attract hate and despair. The young president also learned this the hard way.

Are you ready for what you wish for? Are you ready for success? If we are ready, there will always be a teacher to help us achieve what we want. There is a saying that, *"When the student is ready, the teacher appears."*[61]. In other words, we can have what we want only when we are ready for it. Many of us wish and want things in life only to lose them when they show up in our reality. Usually, this happens because we are not ready to receive it. There are men and women who pray for better relationships in their lives. When that special person comes into their lives, they start complaining of other things the person does not have. *They start focusing on lack.* Look at your life right now and assess it. What are you complaining about? Is it something you had wished for? If so, are you positive, grateful, or ready to receive it? Sometimes, we cheat ourselves from a happy life by looking at the faults of others instead of being grateful for what they bring. This was the mistake of the entire community's townspeople.

---

[61] "When the student is ready, the teacher appears" Gautama Buddha, founder of Buddhism.

There comes a time in a society when the entire society makes a mistake. That is, an individual cannot be blamed for that particular mistake but the entire society. It said that this entire community in this foreign land made a mistake. Not a single person but the entire community. They never recovered to structure their lives the way they wanted after the young president left the land. The young man gave the community his all and made a lot of sacrifices and progress for the people, but many of them became focused on other things he was enjoying from his success. Some focused on his mistakes, and others focused on envying the *Power and Control* he had or enjoyed. The situation became toxic, divisive, and even deadly. Though they made some piece, the atmosphere was no longer habitable for the president. The young president picked himself up and left the entire land. He left his people and community for good. His departure took the community by surprise and by shock. No one believed he could do it. It was also sad! Many people were hurt and frustrated about his departure. It created a despondency in the community. Many members begged for his return and some tried to persuade him to do that. What do you think? What would you do if you were this young man? Will you ever return to that land? What will you do differently? After the president left, did this vibrant community get better, or did it go back to disunity? What would happen after that?

High-Performing Leadership Traits

Leadership

A healthcare organization comprises several very different individuals working together to deliver care to individuals in need. Leadership is essential to the success of a healthcare organization. Leadership is the ability of an individual or individuals to guide others and enable them to reach the goals of the organization. An organization with the ability to recognize and develop strong leaders will create higher levels of success, highly motivated employees, and higher employee retention. An organization comprises several very different individuals, which makes leadership development unique to each individual. Teach qualified individuals leadership skills and develop each individual to become a successful leader. There are several common ways to help individuals transition into leadership roles, including modeling, coaching, and management mentoring.

Modeling is a teaching strategy where individuals learn by behavior modeling or mimicking someone else's behavior (Mathis, Jackson, Valentine, 2014). It is important for leaders to lead by example and actively train employees to be effective leaders in the organization. Leadership training and development are most effective when demonstrated in the real work of the leaders as hands-on trainers (Wells & Hejna, 2009).

Coaching is another effective way to develop new employees or transition existing employees into a leadership role. Coaching combines observation with positive reinforcement and suggestions by incorporating the training process into real work situations (Mathis, Jackson, & Valentine, 2014). Management mentoring is a training method that creates a relationship between experienced managers and less experienced managers to help aid the new individual when developing technical, interpersonal, and organizational skills (Mathis, Jackson, & Valentine, 2014). This method benefits the inexperienced individual by teaching the essential skills of management and leadership, but it also benefits the experienced manager by allowing him/her to demonstrate leadership and management, which will remind him/her of the importance of leadership in the organization.

Leadership Traits

Leadership is a process by which an individual influences others to accomplish the goals of an organization. Leaders express and apply their individual attributes, including their beliefs, ethics, character, knowledge, attitudes, and skills, throughout the leadership process (Wells Hejna, 2009). The ability to recognize individuals with quality leadership traits and develop these individual's traits and capabilities into the culture of the organization is a key factor to a successful organization. David McClelland recognized five traits that high-performing leaders possess, including character, personal capability, focus on results, leading change, and interpersonal skills (Wells & Hejna, 2009).

Character

Character combines one's values and traits that form an individual's nature. Honesty and integrity are part of one's character and are both essential to quality leadership. An individual's character can be developed over time by learning right from wrong and the importance of honesty. This characteristic should be developed earlier in life through a parent or a role model.

Personal Capability

Problem-solving, technical knowledge, innovation, and self-development are all aspects of personal capability traits (Wells & Hejna, 2009). Personal capability traits can be taught and developed; however, the desire to want to self-develop has to come from the individual. Technical skills, finance, and problem-solving can all be taught, but each individual may possess higher/lower capabilities of these traits, so it is crucial to recognize each individual's strengths and weaknesses when developing their leadership skills.

Focus on Results

Goal setting and developing or change and organization a key characteristics of a successful leader. Leaders need to know what direction the organization is headed and how to get it there. Through effective training, potential leaders can develop the courage to take chances and initiate growth.

Leading Change

McClelland describes leading change characteristics as having the ability to develop strategic perspectives, champion change, and connect the group with the outside world (Wells & Hejna, 2009). Change is inevitable, especially in healthcare. Successful leaders recognize the need for change, develop a plan, and set the plan in motion. Leaders provide knowledge and insight about the goals and strategies to reach the goals. Effective leaders provide the staff with the tools needed for change. This characteristic can be taught and developed.

Interpersonal Skills

A leader must communicate effectively to co-workers and employees. Leadership is the ability to guide other individuals and motivate them to want to perform at higher levels. An effective leader builds positive working relationships and inspires others to want to develop themselves. Interpersonal skills are unique to each individual but have the potential to be developed and expanded upon.

Conclusion

This paper explains the importance of leadership and gives a detailed description of how effective leadership is crucial to an organization. This paper discusses the key characteristics of leadership developed by David McClelland and how to develop or teach these characteristics. Leadership traits are important to the success of each individual leader and the overall success of the organization. Leadership is the influence that one individual has on other individuals. Leaders express and apply their attributes to influence others to want to learn, grow, and succeed within the organization.

References

Mathis, R. L., Jackson, J. H., & Valentine, S. R. (2014). *Human Resource Management* (14th Ed.). Stamford, CT: Cengage Learning.

Wells, W., & Hejna, W. (2009). Developing Leadership Talent in Healthcare Organizations. *Healthcare Financial Management, 63*(1), 66-9.

For other information related to this book, visit our website;

⇓⇓⇓⇓⇓⇓⇓⇓⇓⇓⇓⇓⇓

www.100TextMessagesFromaPresident.com